Rosé Exposé

Discovering wine's best-kept secret

2003 edition

STEVE BROADHEAD
&
JAMES HAYES

Rosé Exposé Communications

Rosé Exposé
By Steve Broadhead & James Hayes

2003 edition published by Rosé Exposé Communications.

UK office: First Floor, 19 Avenue Road, St. Albans,
Hertfordshire AL1 3QG.
Tel: +44 (0)709 221 8400
Fax: +44 (0)709 221 8400

France office: La Calade, 1 Chemin de Roquecourbe,
11700 Moux, Aude, France.
Tel: +33 (0)4 68 43 99 70
Fax: +33 (0)4 68 43 99 71

Email: info@rose-expose.com
Internet: www.drink-pink.com

ISBN 0-9545002-0-2

Edited by James Hayes
Photography by Studio Otto

Dedicated to the memory of Maggie Davies

Set in Georgia and Twentieth Century

Printed and bound by Biddles Ltd., Woodbridge Park Estate,
Woodbridge Road, Guildford, Surrey GU1 1DA. Tel: 01483
502224. Fax: 01483 576150. Internet: www.biddles.co.uk.

Contents

It's time for rosé to show its true colours, says Tony Laithwaite

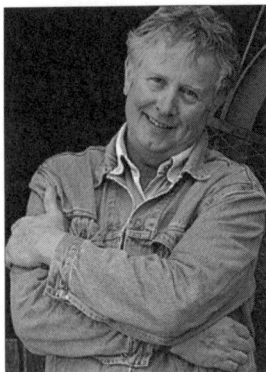

It is indeed high time rosé was accorded equal status with white and red wines. In reality there are no clear-cut boundaries. Virtually all grape juice starts out white, it is some of the skins which contain the red colouring.

If the skins are macerated in the juice, the colour seeps into the wine. From red grapes therefore it is possible to make everything from white to almost-black wine.

Pink wines come in the middle of the spectrum and are extremely difficult to make well... Timing is crucial, and so is a subtle sense of balance. In France, in August, we drink little else — so do most of our neighbours...

I hope my friends (and customers) Steve and James will help you and us to discover many more delights of mid-spectrum wine!

I offer *Rosé Exposé* my heartiest best wishes,

Tony Laithwaite
Chairman
Laithwaites — *'UK's No.1 Independent Wine Specialist'*

"Deep in the hearts of most inveterate wine lovers lies a passion for rosé, though it usually doesn't come up for discussion unless the subject is broached in trusted company."
— Gerry Dawes, *The Wine News*.

Welcome to *Rosé Exposé* — the first book about rosé wine. At a time of a wealth of wine books, it seems odd — even perverse — that pink wines should have been so ignored by wine authorities and the best-buy gurus; yet even ardent advocates of wine inclusiveness seem to have a blind spot when it comes to rosé.

Published partly in response to this glaring gap in the wine guide market, *Rosé Exposé* is intended as an introduction to curious quaffers, and a reference guide for the growing ranks of rosé aficionados.

Rosé Exposé was conceived during a conversation at a PR party in 1999. One of us remarked that although two or three different types of red and white wine were being served that evening, never could we recall having been offered a single rosé. Steve Broadhead, who had already lived in France for several years, pointed out that this would not happen in France, where rosé was integral to social lubrication.

In the ensuing conversation we discovered a shared penchant for quality pink wine; Steve, it turned out, was a convert well before relocating from his native Yorkshire, and James Hayes had been rustling rosé at home and abroad since vacations to the Côte d'Azur in the early 1980s.

We also agreed that we had not come across much more than a footnote or two about rosé's merits in any of the wine books we had read. Why was this?, we wondered. There must be many confirmed rosé fans, and curious wine enthusiasts, who would like to learn more about it. Surely there was scope for celebrating quality rosé in its own right?

It was two years before we found time to develop the idea. During that time our researches for *Rosé Exposé* have confirmed the belief that a 'rosé renaissance' was emerging. We launched a website to support the nascent *Rosé Exposé*, called *DrinkPink* (www.drink-pink.com) —

this has attracted much support from rosé-quaffing quarters around the world. As we had suspected, there were many wine folk who shared our passion for rosé. As a result, *DrinkPink* and *Rosé Exposé* are being extended into additional publishing formats during 2003.

But what do we mean by 'quality' rosé? Well, what we do *not* mean is the bog-standard Portuguese or French rosés that are found (and have been for years) in too many corner shops, off-licences and supermarkets. This pink plonk is, alas, what many wine drinkers base their view of rosé on. There is certainly a market for these wines, and we probably stand guilty of depreciating them without actually having sampled enough of them. But life is short.

By quality rosé, we mean pinks wines that are produced to the same standard as middle- and higher-range reds and whites – and often coming from the same wineries. *Rosé Exposé*'s mission is to alert wine drinkers to *real* rosés: those from winemakers who are dedicated to higher standard ingredients and production methods that are consonant with the production of wines of a recognisably higher quality.

viii They are winemakers who nurture their vineyards carefully, make individual (idiosyncratic or even eccentric) decisions on production procedures, experiment with different grape varieties and percentage blends, and limit their production according to the quality/quantity thresholds they set themselves.

Producers of quality rosés are almost always producers of outstanding red and white wines. They observe no quality differential between the styles; rosé is made with the same care and devotion, just in a different way. And it should be appreciated as demandingly as one would a good quality red or white. In the final analysis, we reckon that anyone with half a tastebud faced with a glass of bog-standard rosé and a glass of 'the real stuff' will not need *Rosé Exposé* to discern the difference; we are just trying to help point them in the right direction...

They will be co-joining a wave of 'vinimania' that seems to have engulfed every facet of wine except rosé. This mystified us – a rosé publication seems an ideal candidate for the wine canon. There is plenty to say about this style of wine.

Rosé's relative obscurity is not ubiquitous. In the main European wine-producing countries like France, Spain and Italy, incidental evidence shows that rosé consumption is on the up. But rosé fans are also forming a growing constituency among UK wine drinkers. This is due to five main reasons:

- Quality rosés are now widely available to UK consumers — for the first time ever.

- Recognition that rosé merits better appreciation and redemption from 'wine snobbery'.

- Interest in matching wine with food — rosé is often better than red or white as a food-accompaniment.

- Rosé is very often better than white or red as a 'quaffing' wine during social situations.

- Rosé 'evangelists' are coming out of the cellar and proclaiming their faith.

There's no denying that rosé has an image problem. This is an inhibitor to its popularity in the UK, and this will be examined later in the book. Associations foisted on rosé by cheap pink plonk have over the decades blighted its reputation. It is amazing just how durable is the misperception that all rosé is sweet, fizzy, and low-alcohol.

Even self-professed wine buffs and seasoned traders can be customarily ignorant about the range and diversity of still pinks: they are surprised that most of the renowned French producers of red and white also produce rosés to the same high order; they are taken aback to learn that rosé regularly wins awards in international wine competitions; they are gobsmacked to learn that top chefs recommend rosé as the best accompaniment for many foods and styles of cuisine; they are delighted that the price of rosé can be half that of reds and whites of comparable pedigree.

The Internet is key to obtaining more and better rosé. Merchants big and small, specialist and general, are exploiting the Net to source and sell superior rosés; it means that they can service low-volume demands that hitherto were insufficient to cost-justify the effort. We list many of these merchants in Chapter 10 and the Appendix to *Rosé Exposé*.

The Net factor is important to getting the most out of *Rosé Exposé*: its authors assume that its readers will have Internet access, or are habitual surfers happy to use the web to buy products and services. We know that even in this 'wired' age of Net 'haves and have-nots', this assumption remains contentious; but without it a book like this would have been obviated. To any 'unwired' rosé fans who feel excluded by this, we can only apologise.

As former computer journalists who have written much about electronic commerce — e-commerce — we believe that the Internet is empowering consumer-driven freedom to find what *exactly* they want, rather than what dominant suppliers think they should want, and all from the comfort of their personal computer.

At its best, the Net enables smart small wine producers and suppliers to flourish in a commercial world increasingly carved up by cartels keen to wrench control of supply chains. The rise of rosé exemplifies the trend toward minority catering. We hope that *Rosé Exposé* will attract more converts to this marvellous liquid.

Vive le rosé!

Steve Broadhead
James Hayes
March 2003

Chapter One

Pink preference

The Cinderella of the wine world

"Which would you prefer – red or white?"

I t's a common enough question; but how often are you offered a third option – rosé? How often have you heard anyone actually ask for rosé?

Rosé is wine's best-kept secret; that's a cliché, but it's true. With more wine books in print than ever before, it is remarkable that even famous appellations like Côtes de Provence scarcely rate a mention in most tomes. Rosés are consumed in great quantities every day around the world – France alone produces an estimated 430m+ litres of rosé each year; it is prized in major international wine awards; leading winemakers esteem it.

Yet quality pink wine is largely blanked by the vinocracy, which has cast rosé as the Cinderella of the wine world; the time is surely ripe to accord it the recognition it deserves.

3

For rosé aficionados, this recognition is long overdue. Finding out about rosés – how they contrast and compare, how they are best appreciated, and where to find the good stuff – has been mostly by dint of individual fieldwork. Information specifically about this style is missing from most wine guides. Many wine merchants arc unknowledgeable on the subject. Enter *Rosé Exposé*, an introduction, guide and celebration of rosé wine.

Part of *Rosé Exposé*'s purpose is blatantly evangelistic. Rosé has suffered an image problem – in the UK at least – for decades. Mention rosé to even well-informed wine drinkers and they will probably grimace and mutter something about Mateus and Rosé d'Anjou tasting like cherryade. To be sure, cheap pink wine has undermined rosé's reputation, as shall be seen, to an extent unfair even by the merciless standards of the wine industry. After all, there is plenty of shoddy Chardonnay around, but nobody assumes that it is typical of the style.

To dismiss rosé as being of irredeemably low quality is to do both the wine — and its makers – a big injustice.

Moreover, it prevents us from enjoying some superbly engaging, varied, and delicious wines. Whether you like your wine light, balanced or full-bodied, rosé has a style to suit. And unlike better whites and reds, the superior stuff usually comes at a more affordable price.

There is no contention that the best rosé can achieve the heights of the finest whites or reds. It cannot – mainly due to the processes of making rosé that limit what can be built in to it. However, that still leaves a lot of scope for winemakers to create remarkable bottlings. In any case, how many truly top class whites and reds do we ordinarily drink?

Pink new wave

Rosé generically is being addressed by new waves of winemakers with progressive ideas, who are applying imagination and integrity to what they produce. In many cases, in France especially, the new winemakers include many non-nationals. The term 'flying winemakers' was coined to describe the influx of Australian winemakers into Europe. France has certainly witnessed its fair share of Aussies, but there are also plenty of British, Belgian, Dutch, German and Scandinavian – and a few American – winemakers in France producing excellent wine of all kinds.

Alongside them are many upstart French winemakers who have moved to different regions of France in order to experiment with untried grapes, climatic conditions and wine types. This shuffling of the pack is evolving new ideas, new flavours and – in the case of rosé – many of the bad 'old-school' precepts and habits are being discarded.

Rosé renaissance man — and woman

Thanks to the efforts of this new generation of winemakers, and increasing availability of high-quality rosés via enlightened UK wine retailers and online wine sellers, rosé seems set to enjoy a something of a renaissance. The pleasures of rosé are being discovered and rediscovered. It would be hyperbolic (and factually incorrect) to claim that rosé could become 'the next' Chardonnay or Sauvignon-Blanc; but with adroit marketing, rosé is already en route to becoming the new tipple of choice for trend-conscious imbibers seeking an alternative to the uniform New World reds and whites to which our drinking habits have defaulted over the past few years.

The 'Mateus legacy'

Think rosé, think table lamp or candle holder... That's one of the preconceptions wine-drinkers have about rosé. And, if your palate's sole exposure to pink wine is to sweet, insipid liquid in squat bottles, then it probably also applies to your assessment of rosé to date. As a way of describing true rosé, it's akin to basing your view of animated movies on Disney at its cloying and sentimental worst, while denying yourself the full-on *Shrek* experience.

In the UK, rosé certainly has an image problem to deal with. It has been described as 'party wine that nobody takes to parties', a sign of wine crassness rather than savvy. This is a view that appears pretty well confined to the UK, for in rosé-producing societies, it is assuredly deemed *the* party tipple – versatile and sophisticated, perfect for any foods from light bites to four-course buffets.

You do not have to be a wine historian to discover where this notion comes from. In the UK during the 1970s and 1980s, rosé usually meant either Mateus Rosé, generic Rosé d'Anjou or possibly Paul Masson's pink line – medium-sweet, mass-produced shelf fillers. Better rosés were not easy to find; wine sellers offering a diverse range of rosés were rare.

Even wine buffs who took the trouble to read-up on what they were drinking remained unaware of the existence of rosés that came from the same winemakers producing the whites and reds they enjoyed. The only way to get hold of it was to physically bring it back from abroad.

The fact that Mateus, the Portuguese brand created by Fernando Van Zeller Guedes (1903-1987) in 1942, that shaped popular perception of what rosé is about, represents an undeniable marketing success. It is a success built on a marketing conceit of calling what is strictly speaking a *rosado* by the French name for such wine. Equating rosé *per se* with just Mateus is tantamount to thinking that German wine begins and ends with Liebfraumilch. With more travel within Europe, many wine drinkers are returning from visits to Southern France, Spain and Italy – Europe's leading rosé produc-

ers – having acquainted themselves with the superb rosé offerings of those countries. With increasing availability of rosés via specialist merchants on the Internet, there is no longer any reason why a dalliance with rosé while on vacation should remain a holiday romance.

6   An irony of the image problem is that not long after Mateus was invented, rosé became fashionable as a chic tipple. In the Paris of the late 1940s, rosé was the tipple of choice of intellectual smart set luminaries like Jean-Paul Sartre and Simone de Beauvoir (pictured), partly thanks to the efforts of the Béarn appellation, from the Pyrenees region.

Here, in 1947, after the ravages of war and phylloxera, Henri Meyer founded a co-operative and created a new wine, Rosé de Béarn, which found success in France's metropolitan areas, where there was a Gallic vogue for rosé that coincided with the reawakening of French thought and fashion.

Thanks to some smart opportunism by Béarn (and helped probably by bad wartime vintages), rosé suddenly became the drink of the moment, and its vogue coincided with the rebirth of French culture after the dormancy of the Occupation and immediate post-war period. It brought a welcome splash of colour into a world rendered drab by years of war, shortages and utility. Rosé's late-'40s vogue coincided with Dior's New Look, and in some respects signalled the start of the pink-lined 1950s.

Can rosé re-establish itself as a cult wine, identifiable with lifestyle aspirations? Perhaps so. Other drinks have done this. We have vodka bars and rum bars. In wine terms, what other style can boast better credentials to have cult status conferred upon it? Considered as the radical alternative of the wine world – individualistic, marginalised, anti-establishment – it is an ideal choice for image-conscious drinkers.

Adopting rosé society values

Such questions would seem absurd in the South of France and many other parts of the Mediterranean. On the Côte d'Azur, rosé is drunk by the caseload every day. There, rosé is not subject to second-class status. Infiltrate the trendiest bistros in Cannes, Cassis or Saint Tropez, and you'll see what the chic locals drink with their bouillabaisse or bourride: not white, not red, but pink.

For its fans, such locales inspire the classic rosé image, as they envisage themselves sitting outside a café or bar, on the pavement or in a little square. What is it about rosé that's so evocative of such recollections? If you're a rosé drinker, you'll know the scene. It's late afternoon, you fancy a wine, but nothing too heavy at that time of day, you think rosé...

7

Or perhaps you picture yourself reposing on the terrace of a restaurant, hotel or villa, overlooking the Mediterranean, somewhere on the coast of France, Spain, Italy – or maybe even Morocco, Turkey or one of the Greek islands. It's early evening, still warm as the sun begins to lower in the sky. And it's time to quaff something fresh and fruity – rosé wine time, in other words.

The UK and other northern European countries are increasingly adopting a café culture and, with that, the idea of sipping a refreshing drink, sitting at an outside table, even in the middle of a busy metropolitan centre. Rosé, sold by the glass or *demi-pichet*, is the touch of authenticity such scenarios need.

What does it take to reach the 'tipping point' at which consumers start to band-wagon a social trend? Probably a leap of imagination on the part of bar proprietors and their customers could make new generation of rosé wines becoming the next fashion drink in an English spring/summer. Now is the time to start the trend...

Worldwide trend

Rosé is a global phenomenon. Almost all wine-producing regions of the world create pink wines that are eagerly consumed by their indigenous markets. In Europe, the sector is dominated by France, Spain and Italy; Portugal and Greece, naturally, produce respectable rosés. There's even a Belgian effort – AOC Bourgas – and even stalwart UK wine producers have tried their hands at rosés.

Around the Mediterranean rosé producers include Algeria and Morocco. Near-Middle Eastern countries like Turkey, Israel, and Lebanon make it. Rosés can be found in abundance in Eastern European countries such as Bulgaria, Romania, and Czechoslovakia – and even Russia. South Africa boasts many pink varieties.

Those from Chile, Argentina and Australasia also figure in the ranks. *Rosé Exposé* will be surveying many of these regions in detail, with specific reference to far-flung rosés available to UK wine buyers.

Where it has not been possible to sample wines first-hand, the winemakers' tasting notes have been deferred to, as quoted.

Chapter Two

Ten top Rosé myths

Ten top
rosé myths

Few drinks are surrounded with as much misinfor-
mation as rosé. To help, here is a myth-busting
pink drink primer – the Ten top rosé myths
dispelled...

Myth 1: Rosé is just red and white wine mixed together...

So some of us (might) have tried that particular technique
at parties in the distant past (allegedly). Rosé in fact, apart
from a few untypical varieties, contains no white grape
juice whatever. It is made from red grape juice drawn
from the vat while fermentation is still ongoing, and before it has drawn much colour from the skins.

Winemakers then have a choice. They can allow it to ferment further, before stopping the process and bottling the
wine as a semi-sweet wine, such as Rosé d'Anjou; or they
can let it ferment completely, as they would a dry
white. The rosé production process is explained in
fuller detail in Chapter Three – 'Rosé Making and
Rosé Makers'. It is rare for rosés to be subjected to
oak treatment (which is one of the reasons why rosés
are less expensive than whites and reds), but they do exist.

11

Myth 2: All rosé is sparkling...

It is a testament to the pervasive influence of the Mateus
that this impression persists. Even Mateus is only very
lightly sparkling. It is possible that many newcomers to
rosé get this impression on exposure to pink champagnes,
which are made by blending red and white grape juices.
There are also many good quality effervescent rosés made
in the Crémant style.

Myth 3: All rosé is medium-dry...

Rosés come in all grades of sweetness and dryness —
there's something to suit all palates and occasions. Rosés
also come in a surprisingly wide varieties of colour, rang-
ing from the bone dry Bandol *vin gris* to the deep corals of
new generation South American and South African labels,
using Grenache and Cinsault grapes. That rosé offers a
more widely graduated range between dry and sweet is
soundly argued, but it comes down to individual palates
and tastes.

Myth 4: Rosé is cheap — therefore the quality cannot be very high...

There is cheap rosé, as there are cheap whites and red wines. However, a visit to better-stocked wine retailers will indicate that French rosés at least are among the pricier end of the middle range. The extra care that's been going into the rosé production processes has started to be reflected in retail prices. And the disparity that used to exist between rosés, and reds and whites from the same vineyard, is disappearing. Rosé is no longer a cheap by-product — it is being produced as a fully-fledged high-quality wine in its own right.

Myth 5: Rosé is only a glugging wine; it does not merit higher appreciation...

It is certainly true that rosé makes a good 'drinking' wine - i.e., suitable for occasions where a degree of intoxication would not come amiss. But the reasons for this identification are misleading. Few white and red wines are suited to glugging because their powerful flavours overwhelm and nullify the palate (and the brain) during the course of a prolonged evening's sampling. But rosé's balance of ingredients make it much better suited to prolonged consumption. It has not the 'heaviness' of red (or the hangover-inducing congeners), nor the acidity of white that can discombobulate the gastric system.

12

Myth 6: Rosé has low alcohol content...

Certain lighter rosés certainly average an alcohol content by volume of 10% or lower. But this is certainly not the case of the better quality varieties. Many French and Chilean rosés, for instance, are exceptionally potent, with alcohol by volume (ABV) levels commonly of 13.5% -14.5%.

Myth 7: Rosé must be drunk young; it cannot be laid down...

This is certainly the message of most wine advisors, but it is not incontrovertible. There are a number of rosés — notably Bandol in Provence — that benefit from ageing, and are made to do so. Rarer rosés from the Champagne region, such as Rosé des Riceys, are adjudged to improve after five years in bottle. It may be true that, generally speaking, rosés do not *benefit* from being laid down. The wine does not mature and improve in the same way that some reds and some whites do. However, neither does ageing necessarily have a detrimental effect on the bottle's contents. Rosés are, however, prone to colour loss over time, particularly if stored in light), and some consumers find the grey tinge than can result off-putting, though it needn't affect the wine otherwise.

Myth 8: Rosé lacks class — brought to a dinner party, it would be an embarrassment...

This arises from the misperception that all rosé is low-grade plonk - but gone is the time when this was the only sort available. In the UK low-grade rosé is less commonly found, whereas the shelves are groaning under the weight of substandard whites and reds. Rosé is actually perfect t for dinner parties where the nature of cuisine is not known in advance: it is the ideal accompaniment to a wider range of cuisine (see Chapter Nine, 'Rosé and Cuisine').

Myth 9: Rosé needs sunshine to be best enjoyed...

This myth is, in part, true — nothing complements the rosé experience as well as hot sunshine. Yet this does not preclude its appreciation in less temperate climes. It is also true that you are unlikely to enjoy a bottle of chilled rosé in a draughty British pub in January (assuming, of course, you actually found one serving it). But there are many Spanish and Italian restaurants that proactively re-create the warmth of their native lands behind closed (and draught-treated) doors, where good pinks can be had.

13

Myth 10: Real men don't drink rosé...

The British drinking culture has only overcome its qualms about the supposed compromises to masculinity borne of drinking wine comparative recently; so a pink wine is bound to present some residual image problems in the UK. Even in the US, wine taster Joshua Wesson (for Taste of Vail restaurants) posed the challenge "Are you sexually secure enough to drink rosé wines?" at an event held in 2002.

Wine drinkers from France, Spain, Italy, Chile and Argentina must think any such reservations tantamount to dementia, never mind sexual insecurity... Rosé's alcoholic credentials need no overstatement — with 13+% ABV contents common, it is hardly lacking in potency.

(Never forget that abuse of alcohol is dangerous to health. In all instances, rosé is best enjoyed where sensible and moderate intake is observed.)

Chapter Three

Rosé making and rosé makers

The roots of rosé

Rosé has been produced for hundreds of years, in all the wine-producing parts of the globe. In rosé-rich France, for instance, it was the forerunner to the red wine styles that dominate today.

Rosé was being drunk long before primitive vignerons discovered prolonged maceration and fermentation. The original *clairet* in Bordeaux, from which the generic claret designation for Bordeaux reds takes its name, is still today a French rosé wine appellation.

From being the dominant, mass-produced wine, rosé became relegated to something of a by-product, as red wine production techniques improved and its quality became more attuned to mass tastes. As wine consumption entered the 20th Century, rosé became overshadowed by more fully fermented wines.

The reasoning behind this was evidently simple. Rosé can be produced – and is in most parts of the world – using the same production techniques as red wine. Better still, rosé can be produced, and a better quality red wine result, as part of the same winemaking procedure – a win-win situation winemakers were quick to exploit.

17

The winemaker ends-up with a tank full of drinkable (if not particularly high-quality) rosé wine they can sell on cheaply, while also producing a premium quality red wine using the same raw ingredients. This technique remains popular, although winemakers have found ways to improve the process, and to start sharing some of the reds' 'premium quality' in the rosé's favour.

The rosé making process
To outsiders it is not obvious how this production method works, but it is the one used for just about all the rosés under consideration in this book. From a rosé perspective it's what is known as the 'bleeding' method, or *saignée* – France arguably originated the technique. Like all wine-production techniques, it starts with the obvious task of collecting the grapes – dark grapes.

18

Even to this most fundamental of procedures, changes have occurred, such as automated grape collection. The pros and cons of automation as compared to hand-picking, are one of winemaking's many stalks of contention. Individual winemakers apply their own idiosyncrasies to ensure the grapes are delivered to the winery 'just so', as will be seen later.

Then the grapes – grape types that make red and rosé – are crushed, the skins broken so that the juice and pulp are released, and pumped into vats – normally of steel (typical examples from Bodegas López in Argentina are pictured above). Even the way in which grapes are best crushed provokes debate; some winemakers prefer only some of the grapes – those at the bottom – to break initially by the weight of those above. Seasoned rosé makers have their own preference, and can differ markedly.

So starts the natural process of fermentation as the yeasts that live on the grape skins are in contact with the pulp and start to turn the natural sugar (about 30% of the pulp is sugar) into alcohol and additionally create carbon dioxide gas.

To produce solely red wine, this process would continue for typically 10-to-14 days, until all the sugar is converted into alcohol; or at least until the latter level is high enough to kill the yeast and thereby end fermentation.

However, by 'bleeding-off' some of the juice in the early stages (often within a few hours) of fermentation into a second vat, not only is rosé wine created – essentially red without the same penetration of colour and flavour from the skins – but also the remaining fermenting red becomes more concentrated as the juice to skins ratio changes.

In some varieties, more red wine grapes are then added to the red fermentation vat to increase the quantity and 'balance' the resultant red wine flavour. So, not only does the winemaker end up with a more concentrated red wine, but also a vat of fair rosé wine, often to be sold cheaply without even being bottled. Production costs of the rosé were therefore very low — a true 'value-added' by-product.

The period between the grapes entering the vat and bleeding-off greatly determines the nature and character of the rosé produced; as mentioned, this period can vary from a few hours to a day. Like reds and whites, rosés can be made from all the same grapes or from combinations of varietals grown on different *terroir* types. These can be further blended with juices that have undergone different maceration periods. Winemakers will experiment with different periods, grape varieties and blend percentages, until they evolve a wine that they feel is in character unique to them. The scope for variation is almost infinite.

As said, this *saignée* method is the most popular way for producing rosé wine; and it is still making a lot of light, fresh – but unmemorable – rosé wine. For a long time, rosé was victimised by its own success. With a passable product contenting different levels of the consumer market, winemakers had little incentive to tinker with the status quo.

There has always been demand for high-quality rosés, to be sure – for rosés made with the same evolutionary zeal, passion and commitment customary to premier reds and whites. Discerning wine drinkers are always responsive to quality, no matter what colour it comes in.

Making rosé better

By varying the amount of time the grape skins remain in contact with the juice (and the grape varieties themselves, blending them red wine-style after fermentation), higher-class and more individual rosé wines can be created. Many contemporary winemakers are now reviving this age-old process, as interest in a rosé and its 'renaissance' gathers pace.

The addition of computer-controlled fermentation vats – often made of stainless steel – means that winemakers can manage the development of rosé wines to a much more precise degree than before, and thereby get multifarious pink wines, in terms of scent, flavour, colour, and quality. This flexibility and versatility is what is needed in order for a 'new generation' rosé market to be defined, supplied and sustained.

20

First blush of youth

The *saignée* method is not the only way of producing better rosé. An alternative is to separate the juice from the skins before fermentation to get a lighter 'blush' style rosé, such as those popularised by the US, among others, in recent decades. Another is direct pressing, where the grapes are not pre-crushed, but are sent straight to a press and the juice extracted in a single stage.

The arguments in favour of the latter technique revolve around the 'freshness' that is captured from the grapes, like the difference between crushing a whole grape in your mouth, rather than a half that has been sitting around for a few minutes first: a surprising amount of colour can be extracted in this way, too.

Pink wines produced via these methods tend to be less alcoholic and have less body than traditional rosé. Popular in North America, they constitute a niche market elsewhere. Europeans tend to dismiss blushes as scarcely worthy of notice; but there is no doubting the popularity of the mass-market brands. Whatever their relative merits, they are not what this book is about.

New thinking on grape varieties and blending

As rosé has moved on from being just a by-product of red wine, so the grapes used to create it have become more specialised. While it is logical that grapes that make red wine can make rosé also, given the production techniques described earlier, not all red wine grapes make good, or even palatable, rosé.

Many of the heavier, more tannic, red wine grapes such as the Auxerrois (also called Côt or Malbec) and Tannat in France, the Nebbiolo in Italy and the Tempranillo in Spain make excellent red wines that age well, but are less than ideal for a vivid, lively rosé style (although are used for pinks). Instead, rosé winemakers have focused on a subset of grape varieties – often specific to a given region – that make excellent rosé.

Contemporary winemakers are finding opportunities to create new and exciting rosés by blending unaccustomed grapes in finely-tuned percentages; some are bring together more varietals into the mix. Château **21** Romanin, for example, from winemakers Jean-Pierre and Collette Peyraud, and Jean-André Charial, based in the Baux de Provence appellation area, has five — Counoise, Syrah, Grenache, Cabernet Sauvignon and Cinsault – resulting in a spectacularly complex and flavour-driven concoction.

In the Languedoc-Roussillon area of France the Carignan and Mourvèdre grapes (the former plentiful, the latter dark and 'dangerous') are often seen together in red wines, including particularly fine examples, but the latter especially is rarely used in rosé, and Carignan only as part of a blend.

Instead, the Cinsault, Grenache and Syrah grapes tend to be the mainstay of rosé wine production, and all regularly feature as either the primary grape (in blend percentage) or the sole varietal. Cinsault, especially, is a rosé specialist grape, having excellent acidity and colour, flowery, fruity aromas and a brittle skin that cracks easily and is therefore suited to the direct pressing technique that some winemakers employ to crush the grapes.

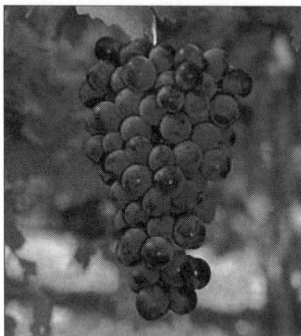

Sometimes environmental factors govern whether a grape will make good rosé in one country, but not in another. Merlot, for instance, is a prime (and sometimes sole) component of pink wines from Chile and Argentina, but not in France, because of the climatic and soils of South America enable it to imbue its juices with the spiciness and minerality apposite to rosé flavour. Grenache, under the name of Garnacha (pictured), is Spain's specialist rosé wine grape, having high natural alcohol levels under fermentation and being prone to oxidisation, producing a paler colour over time. However, Spanish rosado makers are just as interested in experimentation as any makers of pink wine.

Both qualities are ideal for rosé wine production, less so for producing a mid-weight but dark-coloured reds, which is why Grenache or Garnacha is often blended in red wine production to create top-class wines, notably from the Rhone valley in France. Cabernet-Sauvignon is also a popular choice for Spanish rosados.

In California, to produce the blush interpretation of rosé, the native Zinfandel grape is far and away the most popular variety used. Again, it is for the reasons of colour, acid and fruit level, that 'Zin' is used instead of the many other – mainly of French origin – varieties available. It also helps to create a more distinctive wine in its own right.

Turn to the end of this chapter for guides to the Main French rosé grape varieties (page 30), and Associating French wine regions (AOC and AOVDQS) with primary grape varieties (page 32).

Château Romanin – www.romanin.com

Pink pioneers

I n France, progressive thinking on the profile and production of rosé's 'new-wave' extends from small winemakers to bigger drinks companies: here are some makers and shakers to watch out for...

Domaine Des Chandelles, Corbières, Languedoc-Roussillon, France

At Domaine des Chandelles, nestling beneath the Montagne d'Alaric in the Corbières region of Languedoc–Roussillon in south-west France, Peter and Susan Munday run a modern winery in a most classic winemaking location. Drenched by the Midi sun, but countered by the cooling Tramontane winds from the north–west, the Mundays produce a gold–medal winning rosé wine, Chais Suzanne, by means of very specific production methods which exploit the climatic conditions and chalky–clay soil.

Though the area is historically renowned for producing huge quantities of mainly red, low-quality wine, a large percentage of wines produced in the Aude valley are of excellent quality. In addition to the still dominant production of red wine, rosé and white wines are appearing in larger numbers, with a focus on quality rather than quantity.

23

This very description is apt to the Mundays, an English couple who have settled happily in the region, producing a very distinctive range of wines, which owe as much to Bordeaux as to Corbières in style, while using local grape types. It may seem strange to the uninitiated that Brits can successfully make wine in France of all places, but in truth the Mundays are far from alone.

All over France there are British ex-pats, often with little experience in winemaking, running successful wineries. In the case of the Mundays, their prior experience was simply related to drinking the stuff, not making it. But with a will to learn and a deal of effort, the Mundays sourced as much information as they could about winemaking, added their own intuition and the services of an oenologist (wine consultant) and started winning medals for their wines.

Care and attention to detail are key axioms where the production of Chais Suzanne rosé is concerned. The first rule they employ is an ultra-low yield of grapes to guarantee rich, full grape production. Whereas the Corbières yield limit is 50hl per hectare, at Domaine des Chandelles, this is restricted to just 23hl per hectare.

The second rule they employ is when picking the grapes, in this case a blend of 60% Cinsault, and the remainder Syrah with just a smattering of Maccabeu. Here the only method used is hand picking of the whole bunch, which is then transported in very shallow plastic trays, holding just 10kg of grapes, from the vineyards to the winery.

The reason for this is to ensure that the grapes are not crushed at all prior to the production process, which tends to happen in the classic deep containers used even when hand-picking grapes. This has two obvious benefits as a result of the grape skins not cracking but staying whole and unbroken. One is that there is no possibility of oxidisation from the grape flesh being exposed to the open air. The second is that all the freshness of the grape remains intact – which is ideal for producing a big, fruity rosé wine of this ilk.

24

Most rosé producers use the bleeding or *saignée* method to extract the juice from the grapes, but Chais Suzanne is produced using whole-bunch pressing. This is a variation on the direct-pressing method described earlier in *Rosé Exposé*.

In this instance, entire bunches of grapes, (with stalks on to create more space for the grapes to crush, and release their juice) are pressed directly and the resulting juice – fresh and zesty, with an intense but dark (not blush) pink hue – is fermented at a very low temperature to ensure maximum freshness and natural acidity retention (vital in order to produce a lively edge to the wine) through blocking malolactic fermentation.

The wine has a delicate rosé-pink hue but is full and round in the mouth with a sharp nose and apple and pear drops (like the boiled sweet Spangles) flavours to the fore. It has a long fruity aftertaste with good acidity.

Domaine des Chandelles,
11800 Floure, France.
Tel: +33 (0) 468 790010 Fax: +33 (0) 468 792192

Rutherglen and Beverford Vineyards, Northern Victoria, Australia

While a contingent of fans will insist that pink wines are best enjoyed amid blazing sunshine, excessive rays are not conducive to growing the right vines for rosés.

While vignerons in the South of France may feel they work with plenty of sun on their backs, often what they experience is nowt compared to that of an Aussie winemaker.

Take R.L. Buller & Sons in North-West Victoria, where temperatures annually are expected to range between 10-40°C. Great for producing ripe grapes, but how ripe do you want rosé wine grapes?

Buller's answer is to make sure the rosé is always the first wine made from any vintage, picking the grapes in March and bottling in May – after maturation in stainless steel tanks – to preserve all the fresh, fruit flavours they are searching for.

25

The Buller family has been growing vines since 1921. According to Richard Buller, the company's rosé wine sales are increasing all the time, to the extent that production of rosé has been increased to cope with demand. "I believe that this latest release will please our regular customers and… win over some new customers who have, until now, passed rosé by."

Buller's Victoria 2002 Rosé is lighter than most modern French styles at just 11% ABV – ideal for blazing hot Australian summer days – and is described as having "bracing acidity, good length", with tropical fruit scents on the nose and ripe grapes with tropical fruit, pineapples and plums in the mouth. It is intended to be drunk young, with no proclaimed ageing potential. Victoria 2002 Rosé was awarded a Bronze Medal in the 2002 Royal Perth Wine Show.

www.buller.com.au

Domaine de Jarras Listel

Whereas Domaine des Chandelles is a relatively small (30 hectares in total) private winery, our next French example of state-of-the-art rosé wine production is a giant.

Listel, based in and around the Languedoc, Provence and Rhone areas of France, has over 3,600 hectares of vines and produces Europe's best-selling rosé wine in the form of its Listel Gris (pictured), effectively the equivalent – colour-wise – of a Californian 'blush'. Founded in 1883, Listel is the largest private wine producer in Europe. It specialises in light wines that are ideal for matching wine-unfriendly food, such as Indian cuisine.

Its Grain de Gris is an exceptionally pale, salmon-pink rosé, made from a blend of Grenache, Carignan and Cinsault grapes, which undergoes no maceration whatsoever, but is direct pressed, which helps give the pale colour. It is made to be drunk throughout an entire meal – not something easily achieved with reds or whites – or as an aperitif.

www.listel.fr

Domaine Baillat, Corbières, Languedoc-Roussillon, France

At the foot of the south-facing slopes of the Montagne d'Alaric in the Corbières, Christian Baillat has a focused and single-minded approach to wine growing.

The old Baillat family estate was modernised in 1985 since when the five original hectares of planted vines have been expanded to 13. So a combination of old and new vines are used in the wines, but with more concentrated fruit than before.

Christian's aim is to bring the *terroir* into his wines rather than change the nature of the land to suit his idea of what a wine should taste like. So the Baillat wines are made without compromise, reds and rosés alike.

Consequently, for his Domaine Baillat Corbieres AoC Rosé, while the mix of grape types (60% Syrah, 30% Cinsaut, 10% Grenache), and the *saignée* production method stays the same year-in, year-out, the style varies depending on the particular harvest. For example, while his 2000 vintage – an excellent rosé vintage in the Languedoc – saw overnight maturation produce a deep-hued, full-bodied rosé, though beautifully balanced, with acid and fruit, his 2001 – a lighter vintage – saw a shorter maceration resulting in a livelier wine, drinking earlier than its predecessor, in an easier-drinking style with some *pétillance* still in the mouth.

www.baillat.com

Château de Sours, Bordeaux, France

Esme Johnstone (pictured above) who runs Château de Sours in Bordeaux was the founder of the Majestic Wine Warehouse chain in the UK. In 1990 he took over the Château and 30 hectares of vines, on a site where the first vines were planted in 1792.

Primarily from Merlot grapes, Château de Sours Rosé is created using the *saignée* method and is then cold fermented for 8-10 weeks. It has a vibrant reddish-pink colour – deeper than many rosés. The 2002 is noted as being particularly concentrated as the Merlot crop was 30% down on normal levels, hence the relatively dark hue.

Johnstone describes the colour extraction from the skins as being "almost instantaneous", a description equally applicable to the fruit extraction. A fairly weighty rosé at 13% ABV, the wine carries four grams of residual sugar which will help it age gracefully for a couple of years.

Whenever and wherever Chateau de Sours Rosé is mentioned, so it is accompanied by the late Auberon Waugh's quote (from the *Telegraph Magazine*) about Johnstone having chanced "upon the best rosé in the world"; a lot to live up to!

Also described as "a rosé for wine drinkers who think that they don't like rosé", seasoned rosé buffs might beg to differ on this point. This is certainly a challenging wine and one that rosé fans especially should find immensely enjoyable. Château de Sours Rosé has become increasing available to UK outlets, including Majestic and Tanners.

Distinctively richly dense in body and colour, it is admittedly on the way to becoming a light red wine, hence the "rosé for non-rosé fans" tag, presumably. The 100% Merlot content gives it a real distinctiveness and *gravitas*, but the aroma and flavour does not 'burst out'. Acidity is well-balanced and agreeable.

The bouquet is sedate and unlike the poppy, peppy fragrances most associated with French rosés — in some respects it more resembles a Spanish *rosado*. Up-front flavours of stewed smoked fruit (if you can imagine that), powerful and lasting.

Château de Sours Rosé has been described as having "easy-drinking charm", but it's a much bigger wine than that phrase suggests it might be. Certainly, its style would make it a good accompaniment to lighter, sweeter red meats such as rabbit, venison, and wild boar, as well as smaller game (pigeon, quail, guinea fowl). It would be equally at ease with spicy cuisine, though we challenge anyone to find Château de Sours rosé on any Far Eastern restaurant wine list.

As a relevant aside here, we felt that it was quite demanding in terms of its preferred temperature. It seemed to get recalcitrant if it wasn't chilled just-so, which means it has to be handled by savvy sommeliers — high street Tandoori or Peking restaurants please note.

www.chateaudesours.com, www.majestic.co.uk, www.tanners-wines.co.uk

Domaine de la Perdrielle

The Loire has not always had a reputation for fine rosé wines, but Vincent Gandon at Domaine de la Perdrielle is one of many looking to change that view.

Situated in the Touraine region of the Loire, Gandon makes both still and sparkling rosés – the latter using the traditional champagne method, his father Jacques having studied in the Champagne region and brought his knowledge back with him to good use in Tours.

The local Grolleau grape along with Cabernet Sauvignon make up the *cépages* in this wine, the grapes being hand-picked and transported in small baskets to avoid damage to the fruit before pressing. The result is an onion-peel hue, and a beautifully-balanced wine with lots of fruit, bearing 14 grams/litre of residual sugar – the reason why it is dry but still with sweet fruit in the mouth.

The Domaine de la Perdrielle Touraine-Amboise rosé sec is made up of 45% each of Cabernet Franc and Gamay grapes with 10% Cot. Interestingly the wine is created by a combination of methods – 60% is saignée method, bled-off after a 24-48 hour maceration period, while the remain 40% is direct-pressed. The result is a powerful wine with fruit, flowers and pepper in the mouth, while remaining very lively and moreish. All the Perdrielle wines are made without additives.

Main French rosé grape varieties

Traditionally the grapes used for rosé were the same as those used for making red wine – the rosé being an off-shoot of red wine production. However, this is changing, as winemakers start to select grapes specifically for their suitability for pink wines alone.

Cabernet Franc
Widely grown in Bordeaux, this variety, known locally as 'Breton', produces fruity wines with powerful aromas of red fruit. It is lighter and less tannic than Cabernet-Sauvignon. Cabernet Franc is a grape equally popular in the Loire.

Cabernet-Sauvignon
Cabernet-Sauvignon is the most famous red variety in the world. It is widely planted throughout the whole of France, producing robust and full-bodied wines, which are deep purple in colour and with powerful, blackcurrant aromas and good tannins. Used on its own, its wines age well, particularly those that are matured in oak. Mixed with other varieties (such as Merlot, Syrah and Cabernet Franc), it produces more supple and refined wines, which may be enjoyed younger, including rosés: those made from 100% 'Cab-Sauv' are common.

30

Carignan
Produces full-bodied, intensely coloured wines, which are a good base in blends. Widely planted in the south of France, and used in many rosé blends. Cariñena in Spain.

Cinsault
Used primarily in the production of rosé wines and light reds, especially in the southern Rhône region. Has good acidity and colour and is often used as a blend with Grenache and Carignan.

Counoise
Primarily a blending grape with soft tannins that imparts a peppery accent. Most often used in low percentages.

Gamay
White juice Gamay noir grapes undergo a short maceration process to produce soft, fresh and very fruity red

wines. These very refreshing and easy drinking wines are often sold as nouveau or primeur wines. The Gamay variety is a widely planted red variety and can be found in both the Loire and eastern French regions, and 100%-Gamay rosés exist.

Grenache
Used as a base in blends, this variety gives added alcohol, body and strength and interesting fruity aromas. Popular in most of the South of France. Called Garnacha in Spain.

Grolleau or Groslot
A high-yielding variety, producing red or rosé wines, which are light and lively. Particularly common to the Loire region.

Mourvèdre
Another blending grape, which provides structure, 'backbone', and aging potential to wines. Most often used in low percentages.

Pinot Noir
This early maturing variety is susceptible to frost. It produces red wines and occasional rosés, as well as being the primary grape of champagne. It has very pleasant tannins and aromas of red fruits, which may evolve into animal aromas.

Sciacarello
Undoubtedly the most typical of all Corsican varieties. It thrives on the granite soils and is blended with Grenache or Niellucio to produce full-bodied, red and rosé wines with very fine, spicy and peppery aromas.

Syrah
The Syrah grape is highly prized in the Rhône Valley, this variety positively thrives on the warm and dry climate of Languedoc-Roussillon. Although Syrah was a relative latecomer to the region, it is this variety that has been most instrumental in the evolution of the production of red wines and is commonly used in rosé production. Its success is such that it is fast becoming the most important variety in the Pays d'Oc. Rosés consisting of 100% Syrah are common. This grape variety is also widely known as Shiraz elsewhere in the world, and as such, is as famous as a wine brand as it is as a component part.

Associating French wine regions (AOC and AOVDQS) with grape varieties

New World wines are generous in providing label detail about grape types; in France this is relatively uncommon. This guide helps predict what grapes might be found in the mainland French rosés. The primary grape types that can be associated with a rosé from that region are given.

Alsace
Pinot Noir

Cabernet d'Anjou
Cabernet-Sauvignon, Cabernet Franc

Côteaux d'Aix en Provence
Grenache, Cinsault, Syrah, Mourvèdre, Tibouren, Braquet

Arbois
Poulsard (AKA ploussard)

Bandol
Grenache, Cinsault, Syrah, Mourvèdre, Tibouren, Braquet

Béarn
Tannat, Cabernet-Sauvignon, Cabernet Franc, Manseng Noir, Courbu Rouge, Fer Servadou

Bellet
Rolle

Bergerac Rosé
Cabernet-Sauvignon, Cabernet Franc, Merlot

Bordeaux Rosé, Clairet
Cabernet-Sauvignon, Cabernet Franc, Merlot

Vins de Corse (Corsica)
Sciacarello

Châteaumeillant (gris)
Gamay

Cheverny
Gamay

Chinon
Cabernet Franc

Côtes d'Auvergne
Gamay

Côte Roannaise
Gamay

Côtes du Forez
Gamay

Côteaux du Loir
Pineau d'Aunis, Cabernet-Sauvignon, Cabernet Franc,
Gamay, Côt

Côtes de la Malepère, Cabardès
Grenache, Syrah, Cabernet-Sauvignon, Cabernet Franc,
Merlot

Côtes de Provence
Grenache, Cinsault, Syrah, Mourvèdre, Tibouren,
Braquet

33

Côtes du Rhône/Villages
Grenache, Syrah, Mourvèdre, Cinsault,

Côteaux Varois
Grenache, Cinsault, Syrah, Mourvèdre, Tibouren, Braquet

Côteaux du Vendomois
Pineau d'Aunis

Fief Vendéens
Gamay, Cabernet Franc, Pinot Noir

Gaillac/Côtes du Frontonnais
Negrette, Côt, Cabernet-Sauvignon, Cabernet Franc,
Fer Servadou, Syrah, Gamay, Cinsault

Irouléguy
Cabernet-Sauvignon, Cabernet Franc, Tannat

Rosé de Loire
Gamay, Pineau d'Aunis, Grolleau, Cabernet-Sauvignon,
Cabernet Franc

L'Orléannais Gris
Meunier

Languedoc-Roussillon (inc. Costières de Nimes, Côteaux du Languedoc, St. Chinian, Minervois, Corbières, Côtes du Roussillon, Collioure)
Carignan, Grenache, Cinsault, Syrah, Mourvèdre

Marsannay
Pinot Noir

Reuilly
Pinot Gris, Pinot Noir

Rosé de Riceys
Pinot Noir

Rosé d'Anjou
Grolleau

Saint-Pourçain
Gamay, Pinot Noir

34

Sancerre
Pinot Noir

Tavel
Grenache, Syrah, Mourvèdre, Cinsault,

Touraine
Pinot Gris, Pinot Noir, Pinot Meunier

Touraine-Amboise
Grolleau, Gamay, Côt, Cabernet-Sauvignon, Cabernet Franc

Touraine-Azay-Le-Rideau
Grolleau, Gamay, Côt, Cabernet-Sauvignon, Cabernet Franc

Touraine-Mesland
Gamay, Cabernet Franc, Côt

Valencay
Pineau d'Aunis, Pinot Noir

Chapter Four

Europe

Rosé has been produced in Europe since the earliest winemaking times; wine historians believe that rosé was indeed the *de facto* wine for our ancestors before processes of fermentation and maceration were fully evolved. Rosés exist in all the wine-producing nations of Europe, but this chapter concentrates on the principals – France, Spain, Portugal, Italy, and the Eastern European states.

France

It's the most prolific rosé-producing nation on Earth, and Provence is the biggest rosé-producing region therein.

We're talking France, of course, where wine is still drunk with most meals traditionally, often cheap, bone-dry rosé served straight from the wine box or 'cubitainer' to the jug, which gets its fair share of refills. This is a hugely popular lunchtime drink, it being relatively alcohol-light. It is often slightly apple-flavoured, maybe with a hint of red cherries, and ideal with unfussy French lunchtime restaurant food such as *moules-frites* or pizza; 'snack' wine for snack food.

37

With such a broad geographic spread of rosé production, French pinks vary in character and quality as much as any other French wine. They display a strong sense of their regional origins, whether that be Bordeaux, Burgundy or Bandol. This is partly due to a number of rosé-only appellations having been set up, Bordeaux and Bergerac among them. Even the Champagne region has a (still) rosé — Rosé des Riceys AC, made from Pinot Noir grapes. Regarded as being one of the most prestigious (and expensive) rosés, it is rarity even in France.

Again at the upper end of the market, the most famous rosé in the south of France takes its name from the village its production is centred upon – Tavel. Situated in the heart of the Rhone valley, to the northwest of Avignon, Tavel gives its name to a big-bodied, dry wine with tangy flavours, and perhaps less of the fruit characteristic of other rosés of the surrounding areas. Tavel is made primarily from Grenache, Syrah and Cinsault grapes, like the nearby Châteauneuf-du-Pape red, Tavel is traditionally designed to be aged, and will typically improve for a year or two in the bottle.

Tavel is justly proud of itself. It is the only rosé to be found on all the wine lists of all the French three-star restaurants. It has also figured in the favourite lists of many notorious wine drinkers. Author Ernest Hemingway, for instance, was a fan of rosé generally, but had a particular penchant for Tavel. The hard-drinking novelist reportedly enjoyed two or three bottles a day while in France (switching to Spanish rosados during his sojourns south of the Pyrenees).

Nearly all of the Provençal region has produced rosés of note. The names of Bandol, Coteaux d'Aix-en-Provence, Les Baux-de-Provence, and Côtes de Provence are synonymous with high-quality wines in the pink style – often presented in the famed *flûte à corset* bottle (pictured right). The grapes used – primarily Cinsault, Grenache and Carignan – are stalwarts that thrive in the Côte d'Azur climate. Some winemakers experiment with Cabernet-Sauvignon, Mourvèdre, and Syrah.

To the south-west of Provence is Languedoc-Roussillon. This region is a good source of much medium-priced rosé, that is growing in stature in terms of quality. Its better offerings are aspiring to, and even exceeding, the qualities embodied by those of their more illustrious neighbours. The rosés from the La Clape sub-appellation of Côteaux du Languedoc, lying east of Narbonne, are especially interesting. The Minervois region also produces some extremely refined pinks. Much of the rosé produced in this area is classified as Vin de Pays, and notably Vin de Pays d'Oc, a less restrictive designation than Appellation Contrôlée (AC), allowing more and different grape types to be used. Most producers rely heavily on Syrah, Grenache, Carignan, Cinsault and Merlot or combinations thereof. Neighbouring appellation, Saint-Chinian is now turning out fresh and vibrant rosés.

Though a wine associated with warm climes, almost as much rosé comes out of the north-central region of the Loire as comes out of Provence. Because the Loire growing season is relatively long and cool, its pink wines are generally both fruitier *and* more acidic than Provençal ones. There is the unfussy, slightly sweet Rosé d'Anjou — wines so named are sometimes castigated by 'serious' rosé fans, rebuking the region for having produced a lot of pink plonk, but there are better-quality d'Anjous well worth trying. The drier, cleaner and more herbaceous Cabernet d'Anjou, and the dry Rosé de Loire and Touraine Rosés, are must-tries if encountered. These latter wines are not the easiest to find outside France, however.

Corsican wines in general were disparaged and not even found on the French mainland, but its rosé is often cited as the redeeming factor in the island's output, those of Terra Vecchia made from the local varietal Sciaccarello being regularly singled-out for praise. Now the Corsican wine industry is thriving, with many of the best examples being exported – the domestic (mainland) market being still a bit *sniffy* about them. In the UK, Corsican rosés are rare: the Nicolas chain has carried one or two. Notable names to look out for are Vin de Corse AOCs such as Casone, a top of the range selection from the St. Antoine winery at Ghisonaccia, Ajaccio AOCs such as Domaine de Pratavone, based on the popular Corsican Sciacarellu grape and Patrimonio AOCs such as Domaine Giacometti.

Devigne: the rosé specialist

Importer/merchant Devigne Wines describes itself as a 'specialist in rosé', and as such is a UK first. "We're bringing rare, quality French rosés to UK customers who already have a penchant for pink wines," say Devigne proprietors Mike and Pat Robertson. "But we also want to change peoples' view of rosés. Many wine drinkers are under a misapprehension.

"We are sourcing from suppliers who take their rosés very seriously indeed. Our range amply demonstrates the diversity of rosés: some made for drinking young and some – like the Rosé d'Arbois (from the Jura) and the Cabernets from the Loire – made to develop for years."

Devigne's range features 14 pink wines, including unusual vintages. They include a rosé from Arbois in the Jura made from Ploussard grapes (unique to the region), a sweet rosé made with dessert grapes from Cave de St. Sardos (a village near of Toulouse), and an oak-aged Coteaux d'Aix-en-Provence rosé – Cuvée du Temple – from Georges de Blanquet at Château Bas.

www.devignewines.co.uk

Spain

Spain's aridity engenders pink wines that are luscious, deeply coloured, with heaps of body. There are two types of pink wine in Spain: rosado, the pale- and clarete, the darker-pink variety. Though the latter is rarely retailed in the UK, there are good rosados to be found here.

The Rioja region's pink wines are the best known outside of Spain. Other regions benefiting from external development funding are starting to show rosado vintages. Dry rosados mainly from the Garnacha (Grenache) grape, are produced in the north-central part of the Navarra region.

Torres, Marqués de Caceres and Chivite Gran Fuedo are three of the best-known Spanish pinks in the UK, stocked by supermarkets, multiples and independents alike. Oddbins, alongside these two, last year (2002) introduced Capçanes Rosat, D.O. Montsant, a delicious hearty rosado – see separate box overleaf.

40 Majestic, meanwhile, stocks Muga Rioja Rosado – unusually pale for a Spanish wine, very dry, and probably not the best place for a rosado novice to start. Online, there's Laithwaites Ramon Roqueta Rosado Cabernet-Sauvignon and Familia Martinez Bujanda Rosado – bright, mellow and august rosados. Also worth visiting is Rioja Wine Club UK, which offers three Spanish 'rosés', most notably Heredad Bienzoval Rioja from Bodegas Escudero of Gravalos, Rioja Baha. Online seller Compendium Wine Merchants offer Castillo de Liria, Valencia, a non-vintage Bobal rosado, and Mont Marcal, from Penedès. The Sunday Times Wine Club has introduced the fruity San Valero El Bombero Rosado from Cariñena D.O.

There are also some good rosados to be picked-up at small independent outlets in London's Soho: most commendable are the Orvalaiz Cabernet-Sauvignon rosado from Navarra sold at Gerry's Wines & Spirits (74 Old Compton Street, London W1V 5PA); and Condesa de Leganza, a 100% Tempranillo grape rosado from the Finca los Trenzones, Toledo, from Soho Wine Supply in Percy Street.

www.riojawineclub.co.uk, www.oddbins.com, www.majestic.co.uk
www.compendiumwines, www.sohowine.co.uk,
www.sundaytimeswineclub.co.uk

Capçanes Rosat, D.O. Montsant, 2001

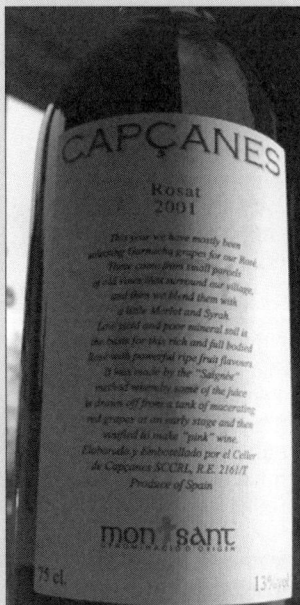

Montsant D.O. is a recent designation, created in August of 2001 as a new Catalan appellation of origin. Before, this winemaking region was sub-region Falset within the DO Tarragona.

Capçanes itself is set high in the 30 miles inland from Tarragona, 100 miles to the south of Barcelona. There has been great investment at the bodega. New cellars have been built to accommodate the new temperature-controlled stainless steel fermentation tanks and 600 new oak barrels have been added, of which about 30% are French-built.

41

Along with the introduction of a new bottling line, there has been much work done on the presentation and packaging of the new breed of wine that is being produced at Capçanes. That this regeneration is paying dividends is evidenced by wines such as the 2001 Rosat. Capçanes Rosat is a mixture of four grape varieties – 65% Garnacha, 15% Tempranillo, 10% Shiraz, 10% Merlot.

The result is a fresh wine of distinctive body and balance, that probably doesn't need to be too well chilled. It arrives on the palate with some force: there's a muted pungency to the flavours, predominantly smoky cherries, deep and very satisfying. The aftertaste doesn't outstay its welcome, but leaves you thirsty for more.

Like many better Spanish rosados, the Capçanes Rosat is sturdy enough to accompany some quite strong cuisines that might otherwise be paired with reds; 13% ABV. It is available from most branches of Oddbins.
www.oddbins.com

Enate Cabernet-Sauvignon Rosado, D.O. Somontano

Idle not to wonder why London's Notting Hill's notorious Portobello Road boasts shops specialising in Spanish produce. Garcia Foods, at 248-250 (tel: 020 7221 6119), is more supermarket than delicatessen, and includes some rosados worth trying if you're in the area antique hunting, carnivalling, or looking to score some grade A pink wine.

Denominación de Origen Somontano is an area in the lee of the Pyrenees, and lies between the perhaps better-known regions of Navarra and Penedès. Somontano is adjudged something of an up and coming region by wine pundits, so rosé buffs will want to sample this relatively unusual offering. Enate is a new, family-owned bodega, founded just eleven years ago. The winemaker, Jesus Artajona, gained his experience working with leading French and Spanish wineries. Its rosado constitutes less than 10% of the output.

Indeed, Enate is something of an arts patron, commissioning labels from painters such as Antonio Saura, Eduardo Chillida, José Beulas, Salvador Victoria, Vicente Badenes, José Manuel Broto, Pepe Cerda, Enrique Torrijos, Alberto Carrera and Frederic Amat. The rosado image is by Victor Mira. Examples of these can be viewed on the accomplished Enate website – www.enate.es.

This is a peppy and engaging pink, its spicey notes shot through with piquant fruitiness, heavy with notes of redcurrants or cranberries – depending on the vagaries of your palate. As noted on the label, Enate rosado has good structure, but its viscosity is somewhat light, and acidity, to our palates, was a little too evident.

So although this is intriguing, it still lacks depth compared with counterparts from neighbouring regions. However, we should also add, this is a lively and enjoyable wine any rosado *entusiasta* should try, despite a relatively

Heredad Bienzoval Rosado

Along with the Campolosierpe Navarra Rosé (1999 – now discontinued), this wine was the rosé opener for Graham Cooke's Rioja Wine Club, and a darn good choice it was too.

Some Spanish rosés can seem to lack body and aroma for the first couple of glasses, before you realise that a cumulative process is taking effect, and a delicious 'cloud' of flavour envelopes the mouth and gullet. This 100% Garnacha-variety wine tends in this direction, but to expect too much from it is too appraise it unfairly.

At their best, Navarran rosés are almost (but not quite) a match for their Northern neighbours. With a bit more encouragement, the Heredad Bienzoval could deliver the extra all-round oomph it needs to really make a mark. ABV is 11.5%.

www.riojawineclub.co.uk

Italy

Like France, Italy produces some very light and very heavy pinks. The naming of such wines can seem confusing: rosato is a form of blush wine, and chiaretto is how the rosé counterpart is labelled. Some chiarettos seem to be labelled as 'rosatos' for export, presumably for branding reasons. Wines of both kinds are to be found along the Italian wine region route.

Pinks are produced in Veneto, said to be Italy's most diverse wine region, but more distinctive Italian rosatos hail from the Salentino area of the Puglia region, where the Negroamaro and Malvasia Nera grapes predominate. These tend to be delicate, flowery, and are some of the few Italian pink wines that improve with age, though their makers recommend early consumption. These wines are hard to come by in the UK. Indeed, some commentators declare the Salento rosati as the best wines from these grapes, possessed of exceptional depth of flavour. Most local DOCs cover this style; a number of producers also make a Rosato del Salento, and a 80% Negroamaro, 20% Malvasia Nera blend split is typical.

Italian pinks seem to be an endangered species to UK consumers. Some tasty Italians that were enjoyed during last summer (2002) seem to have taken flight this year: in particular the Saverio Puglia Rosato late of Laithwaites' list, and the Cavalchina Bardolino Chiaretto from Majestic. Let's hope they will return soon. Meanwhile, Sunday Times Wine Club Members can avail themselves to a rosato from Paolo Masi, scion of the Masi Renzo wine family. It is made from 100% Sangiovese grape, with typically delitescent bouquet and svelte body.

There is also a number of mass-produced Italian 'rosés' on UK shelves under supermarkets' own-brand labels. Although it's unusual to find good Italian rosatos alongside them – or even in specialist delicatessens – at least one usually appears on pasta and pizza restaurant wine lists, such as the Tuscan Marchesi de'Frescobaldi or Rosapina Marche.

Mention should be made of rosatos from Sicily and Sardinia. While a little lacking in finesse, these can be hearty and satisfying, and do crop-up in the UK. The ASK pasta/pizza restaurant chain (part of ASK plc – www.askcentral.co.uk) sometimes has a Rosato di Sardinia as its house pink, and Sainsbury's has the very good Inycon Rosé, Cabernet-Sauvignon Sicilian rosato in selected stores.

Arcadia Rosato Veronese

The branding of this Safeway offering – the label image copied from some old engraving given a 'burnished copper' background – is a bit fusty, and unlikely to pull younger rosé drinkers who could really get into this zesty and easy-drinking wine. The puff on the rear label, alas, doesn't really do the wine justice: quote: 'Inspired wine maker Carlo Corino has created a range of superb, modern wines, combining international appeal with a uniquely Italian flavour...Bright, deep pink colour... reflects the soft, red fruit flavours', and so it blahs on. This purple prose should really be banging on about what an excellent and redoubtable and affordable rosato Arcadia is. The 'fruit flavours' and are very well balanced — the tendency among some of its peers to be steeped in 'strawberry' flavours and odours is resisted, allowing the wine to retain a clean, fresh aftertaste – ideal for party partaking. Rosato

Portugal

Ironically, despite the fact that Portugal has borne two of the most recognisable pinks in the history of wine — Mateus and Lancers – better quality rosados are few and far between. As the Portuguese wine expert and author Giles MacDonogh has observed for the *DrinkPink* wine website, "It takes a brave man to make serious rosé in Portugal — and, alas, they are not many." An exception to this is the famed winesman Dirk Niepoort, whose recent Redoma pink has won high praise. Other Portuguese winemakers experimenting with what is sometimes described as 'new generation Portuguese rosados' include Nuno Cancela de Abreu, who make small quantities of Quinta da Giesta in the Dão region.

In the Estremadura region to the north of Lisbon, Australian Peter Bright makes a pink Cabernet Sauvignon with distinctive grape character ("very sappy", according to MacDonogh), reserving the hulls for the red wines.

In nearby Almeirim, the heirs to D. Luis de Margaride also make a strawberry scented dry rosado from Castelão and Trincadeira. Outside the town is the huge Quinta do Casal Branco where the Lobo de Vasconcellos family – cousins of the Guedeses of Ma-

45

Veronese might have to try hard to accompany a full-blown Italian cuisine; for lighter Italianate meals, it should prove ideal – but it needs to be kept properly chilled throughout.

Despite its rather staid image, this wine could have massive 'yoof' appeal. Its subtle lightness, plus its 11.5% ABV content, make Veronese a perfect wine to accompany an evening session out drinking with friends, yet it would be astounding if you can buy this wine at any UK watering hole. Yes, one could always smuggle some bottles in and consume them in the snug bar away from the bouncers' gaze, but that's hardly the point...www.safeway.co.uk

teus — used to supply Sogrape with grapes for their brands. They now bottle their own wines, and make rosados of a very different style.

So despite the generally mediocre provenance of most Portuguese 'Mateus-wannabe'-pinks squatting on the shelves of supermarkets and convenience stores, some is of surprising quality and drinkability.

Greece

In the same way that Portugal has struggled to allay associations cast by Mateus, so Greek wines are struggling to shrug-off the retsina reputation. Good Greek rosés are not numerous outside their native land, and many Greek restaurants for some reason eschew them on their wine lists.

A retail exception is a redoubtable Greek rosé named Amethystos (available in the UK through Oddbins), produced by Constantin Lazaridis in the city of Drama. Made from 100% Cabernet-Sauvignon grapes, it is dark, dry, and delicious, with an ABV of 12%. Amethystos won a Médaille D'or at the 2000 Montreal wine festival.

46

Just as *Rosé Exposé* went to press, Oddbins added another Grecian wine — Gai'a Agiorgitiko 14-18h

(pictured). It comes in a long tall bottle that risks making it look like chilli oil, but which lends it a certain distinction. The '14-18h' refers to the number of hours that the Agiorgitiko grape skins remained in contact with the juice. Known also as St. George, Agiorgitiko is the principal grape of the Nemea region, and is Greece's second most planted red grape.

Despite Oddbins' laudable patronage, these two Greek rosés are slightly above medium priced. There are a considerable number of Greek regional wines emanating from the many islands that constitute the offshore part of the nation, and sometimes these crop-up on the winelists of Greek restaurants, so do not hesitate to try.

Eastern Europe

There can hardly be a supermarket wine section in the land that doesn't accommodate a pink wine from Bulgaria, Hungary, or Romania. Their drinkability quotient varies, despite the advances made by the respective nations' wine industries; but then, it's unusual to see East European wine of any hue priced over £4, so there should be no surprise at finding a quality deficit.

This is not to say that some of what is available is not well worth trying. A couple of prime examples are Bulgarian Valley of the Roses (from Safeway) and a Romanian, River Route Rosé (sold by Wine Rack) — both profiled below and on the opposite page. Safeway and Waitrose also sell Nagyréde Estate Cabernet-Sauvignon (Száraz Minöségi Dor), from a winery that has received good reports from reviewers.

In the meantime, Fortis Wines of Manchester is selling Lellei Merlot Rosé from Bulgaria, described as having 'delicate strawberry and raspberry aromas [that] give way to a dry, peppery, punchy palate.'

Valley of the Roses Cabernet-Sauvignon Rosé

Valley of the Roses rosé lives up to the description on its rear label: 'Fruity, aromatic... Aromas of crushed strawberries and raspberries'. This is fruity wine, made wholly from Cabernet-Sauvignon grape varietals. But there are other, less easily-definable flavours lurking within this wine, that perhaps have to do with the fact that Bulgaria's Valley of the Roses – in the Maritsa River Valley – is one of the country's most important agricultural regions. It is famed for cropping tobacco, and the production of the oleaginous rose from which attar of roses – a vital ingredient in perfume making – is made. This is designated as Bulgaria's West Sub-Balkan wine region; but the label here does not specify which of the wineries spread around the towns of Karlovo and Maslovetz contribute to this brand. Valley of the Roses has a long-lasting and satisfying flavour, more redolent than its bouquet. It boasts an ABV of 13.5%, but does not seem to carry much of this to the palate or beyond.

River Route Rosé

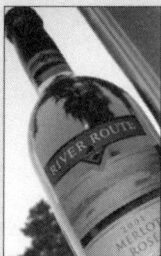

River Route is a respected and award-winning Romanian label, out of the Carl Reh Winery in Bucharest, which also produces the Val Duna and La Cetate brands; but as far as we know, it has no gongs so far for its pink line.

Almost *gris* in its delicate ochre colouring, River Route Rosé is an unfussy but subtly feisty wine, with a savoury, slightly 'smoked' flavour that can take a couple of glasses to make its appeal. However, once the connection had been made, the full flavour of this wine is unlocked.

River Route Rosé has depths that are not exactly hidden but do need to be coaxed out; they may not be apparent from the first taste, but drinkers should persevere. It should prove equally enjoyable with food or on its own; given plenty of time to breath, we think it will also make a passable dessert wine where the fare tends toward the cheese and biscuits rather than sweet puddings. A hearty 13% ABV content.

48

Russia

Russia has long been a significant wine-producing nation, but with little or no export market in the Western world, few outside the old Eastern bloc have tasted its wines. They even have a French-style, tiered quality control system in place, with the AOC equivalent marking out the top wines of the country.

The winemaking is concentrated in the south-west of the landmass, around the Black Sea area where the climate is more approachable to ripening grapes. Even so, Russian growers have experienced very limited life spans of their vines compared with Western European equivalents. Whereas, for example, many French vineyards have a significant percentage of root stock that is of 40 years or older, in Russia they have struggled to get vines to fruit for more than 15 years before replacement stock has been necessary.

Fanagoria

At Fanagoria winery, by the Black Sea, they have been experimenting recently with vine seedlings of high quality
Cabernet-Sauvignon, Ugni-Blanc, and Colombard grape
varieties, purchased in France, in an attempt to increase
the longevity of their vines. Traditionally, the grape types
they use for the rosé wines are somewhat more indigenous, if common in some cases. These include the Trami-
ner – ubiquitous in Germany and Austria – the Moldova,

the Doina and the interesting Muscat Rose (pictured above). All the rosé wines they produce are relatively light in alcohol – 9-11% ABV, and are classed as dry wines intended to be drunk with food such as snails, seafood and poultry.

Tbilivino

In Eastern Georgia at the Tbilivino winery, a medium-dry rosé has been in production since the 1984 vintage. Made from a blend of Cabernet plus local Saperavi and Rkatsiteli grape varieties, the wine is described as being rich and fruity. It is available from online supplier Russian Foods.

www.fanagoria.ru
www.nicolas.com
www.russianfoods.com
www.safeway.co.uk
www.sundaytimeswineclub.co.uk/
www.victoriawine.co.uk/htm/wine_rack.htm
www.waitrose.co.uk
http://secure.ukworlds.com/shopkeeper/fortis

Chapter Five

South America

Great wine is made all over the South America, and the continent's winemakers have staked a major claim within the 'New World wine' ascendancy. Countries like Uruguay and Brazil are starting to aim at the heights of exportable quality and quantity achieved by their southern neighbours Argentina and Chile; a selection of rosés from these latter two will be focused on in this chapter.

Argentina

Argentina is one of the world's largest wine-producing countries, probably the most important winemaking region in South America, with Chile a close second. Until a decade or so ago, its wines were almost unknown outside their native land; output was geared for domestic consumption. Then Argentina's potential came to the notice of international wine investors and developers, and the country has hacked-out a redoubtable reputation for its wines in most world markets. This is impressive given that it was achieved despite 1998's natural catastrophe when the River Elño flooded and almost destroyed that year's entire crop of grapes.

The major part of Argentinean vineyards is located along the country's western flank. They extend for over 2,000 kilometres, from the Cafayate Valley in northern Salta, through central-region Mendoza, to the lower-set Rio Negro Valley, to the south-east, in Patagonia. Mendoza is also the centre of Argentina's wine industry.

Rosés from this part of the world are not common in the UK, so do not pass-up any opportunity to try them.

Malbec is the main Argentinean red grape. Other grape varieties include Spain's red Tempranillo and Garnacha, Italy's red varieties Sangiovese and Barbera, and international stalwarts like Cabernet Sauvignon, Merlot, and Shiraz.

Argentinean winemakers have experimented with each and all of these in their rosés, although pinks are not as commonly produced as they are in neighbouring wine-producing countries like Chile; here is a selective survey of some primary examples.

Finca Flichman

The first vineyards were planted in the area of Barrancas, Maipú, province of Mendoza, some 130 years ago. The Flichman family re-inaugurated the property with the name of Finca Flichman in 1910. They continued working the winery until 1983 when it was bought by an Argentine conglomerate. The next big change occurred in 1998 when the winery was acquired by Sogrape, the Portuguese viniculture group (of Mateus fame).

54

Finca Flichman's Jubilé is a 'fine rosado' made from 62% Cabernet Franc and 38% Merlot grapes. Maceration lasts for one day, and is followed by vinification at 18°C.

www.flichman.com.ar

Goyenechea Bodegas y Viñedos

Goyenechea is one of the Argentinean labels that will be familiar to UK wine buyers. It maintains 130 hectares of grapevines in its property 'Basque Country', bordering the small town of Villa Atuel, on the right shore of the Atuel River. The core Cabernet Sauvignon, Merlot, Syrah and Sauvignon Blanc vines come mostly from Goyenechea's vineyards cultivated in Villa

COMMON ROSÉ GRAPES

i

Top: Cabernet Franc.
Second row: Cabernet-Sauvignon, Cinsault, Carignan, Counoise.
Third row: Grenache, Syrah.
Bottom row: Pinot-Noir, Mourvèdre, Gamay, Grolleau

UNITED COLOURS OF ROSÉ   Rosé Exposé

Above right: it's called pink wine, but its colourings reflect the red range of spectrum. Three wines from the Côtes de Provence region representing the diversity of density and hue from France's biggest rosé region. The pale, almost grey-tinged delicacy of Château La Moutète, from an estate near Toulon, is a blend of Cinsault and Grenache. Domaine St. Benoît is a 100% Cabernet Sauvignon. Between them, the Château Beaulieu Côteaux d'Aix en Provence Rosé in the classic flûte à corset *bottle, blended from Syrah, Grenache, Mourvèdre, Cinsault, Carignan and Cabernet Franc.*

Below right: three French regional rosés Château Thieuley Bordeaux Clairet, 2002; Merlot is the main grape for Domaine de Saint-Antoine, a Costieres de Nimes rosé; a Syrah and Cinsault blend from Corbières, Château du Vieux Parc is a winery based between Narbonne and Carcassonne: its fruitiness is reflected in its rich cerise-orange tinges.

Below: many a French supermarche *will typically offer up to 100 different rosé wines, most from the local and neighbouring regions, but many from all over France.*

iii

iv

Above: Spanish rosados tend toward more full-bodied appearance with gemlike depth of colour. Ramon Roqueta (Pla de Bages D.O.) and Bodegas Orvalaiz (Navarra) — 100% 'Cab-Sauvs' — are brilliant examples. The Condesa de Leganza, a 100% Tempranillo rosado from La Mancha D.O., has more subdued colouring. Left: Cabernet Sauvignon is also the constituent of the Santa Rita 120 (named after the number of patriots who found refuge in the Santa Rita cellars during Chile's fight for independence from Spain in 1814). Right: Los Rosales augments its 60% 'Cab-Sauv' content with 40% Merlot.

UNITED COLOURS OF ROSÉ

Constantin Lazaridis' Amethystos Rosé (Macedonia) is made from 100% Greek Cabenet supposed to impart a 'blue tinge' to its intense ruby hue. Fellow Greek Gaia Agiorgitiko 14-18h is made from 100% Agiorgitilko grapes grown on the slopes of the mountainous Koutsi and Klimenti regions of Nemea. Its name derives from the duration of its maceration period.

vi

Left: two examples of single-varietal rosés. Domaine Bois-Malinge is an all-Gamay Vin De Pays from Gilbert Chon & Fils based at St Julien de Concelles. La Croix de Marthe is a 100% Syrah Vin De Pays Du Gard with marked translucency that causes the colouring to vary from top to bottom.

Below: a quartet of unusual top-of-the range rosés. The Cuvée Du Temple — from Georges de Blanquet at Château Bas, Côteaux d'Aix-En-Provence, uses the best Syrah and Cabernet-Sauvignon grapes, which are fermented at a low temperature to retain their subtlety. This is followed by three months' maturation in oak casks, giving the wine mellow woodiness and additional body. Rosés are rarely stored in wooden casks – one of the reasons why even the finest pinks are less expensive relative to white and red counterparts. Lou Muscadou from St. Sardos (Cave de St. Sardos) is a sweet rosé made from Muscat Noir – normally an eating variety. The Arbois Rosé Ploussard, L'Abbaye, Frederic Lornet, looks dark enough to be a red – not surprising as it is made like a red wine with no saignée because the Ploussard's skin exudes little colour; and as more tannins are retained, this rosé has good ageing potential. Arbois is in the Jura region, and Ploussard is a grape variety unique to the area. Marsannay is the only appellation in Burgundy to make a rosé. This wine – from Pinot Noir grapes – is very pale and gris-like in its translucency, with more ochre tinge than the salmony-pink of the Gamay pictured opposite.

Above: the vineyarded landscapes of Corbières are the largest AC area in the Languedoc-Roussillon region. Grapes for its rosés include Carignan, Cinsault, Grenache, Mouvèdre, and Syrah. Below: Most rosés do not improve significantly by ageing, but neither do they suffer, although their colours are prone to slight fading. They are likely to remain quite palatable, however, if well stored and served.

Atuel from 1900 to 1920. The grape harvest runs from February to end of March.

Goyenechea produces two rosés, one for the home market and one for export: both are made from 100% Merlot grapes. It is available in the UK through online wine retailer Best Cellars. The winemaker's tasting note describes them succinctly as 'Young, aromatic and sensual'.

www.goyenechea.com

www.bestcellars.co.uk

Familia Cassone

The winery of the Cassone Family is located in Mayor Drummond, Luján de Cuyo, in the Southwest of Mendoza. Surrounded by a magnificent Andes landscape featuring the majestic Aconcagua Mountain, its Obra Prima Malbec Reserva 1999 Mendoza red recently won praise from Jancis Robinson as a name to look out for.

The Cassone family arrived in Argentina during the 19th century through Celestino Cassone who came from the Piamonte Region of Italy, a fertile region of wine and wheat plantations. The Cassone family are still the owners of the 90-year-old vineyards.

55

In 1998 Eduardo Cassone together with his wife Florencia Ferreira Funes, and his sons, reinitiated the wine venture by building a small winery.

The elegant and attractive Obra Prima rosé, is made with 100% Cabernet Sauvignon grapes, its brilliant colour the result of the fermentation having a short period in contact with the grape skins. It has 'a floral and fruity aroma... with great balance and strength', the winemaker notes. In addition, it is, according to the Cassone's own words, a 'natural and fresh rosé as is the dawn in Luján de Cuyo, good to share the harmony of those special moments of life'. Serve at 3-5°C.

www.familiacassone.com.ar

Bodegas López

One of Argentina's oldest wineries, the founder of Bodegas Lopez, José López Rivas, hailed from Algarrobo (Málaga) in Spain, scion of a vine and olive growing family. Fleeing Phylloxera, he migrated to Argentina in 1886. Twelve years later he settled in Mendoza, and his winemaking flourished. This maker's Rincon Famoso Rosé is from 100% Malbec grapes (pictured above) through the classical method of moderate pomace maceration and fermentation at controlled temperatures. The winemaker's tasting note states that 'Rincon Famoso Rosé bears a marked fruity aroma, with reminiscences of morello cherries, and an intense and vivacious rose [sic] colour.' With one eye on the 'yoof' market, perhaps, Bodegas López adds: 'It is ideal for young tasters'.

www.bodegaslopez.com.ar

Parra Alta Rosé

Chile's celebrated Concha y Toro is the team behind Parra Alta rosé (see separate entry under the section about Chilean rosés). They established their Mendoza cellar eight years ago after spotting the rich potential across the Andes in Argentina. As well as world-class winemaking know-how — this is made from a blend of gently-pressed Syrah, Malbec and Merlot grapes — Parra Alta rosé benefits from a great vintage. According to its UK seller Laithwaites, Parra Alta is a 'deliciously crisp and versatile rosé guaranteed to revitalise the taste buds' (should they need revitalising).

Jean Rivier Winery

This artisan winery, located in San Rafael, Mendoza, Argentina is a family-owned business started in 1956 by Jean Rivier, a Swiss-French immigrant. It produces some 1,400 cases of its pink wine per vintage. Jean Rivier Assemblage Rosé is 74% Cabernet Sauvignon and 26% Malbec grapes. It is macerated over 16 hours then fermented under low temperatures within 12-14°C for four weeks. The fermentation is delayed by the cold in order to conserve some grains of natural sugars.

Winemaker's tasting notes: 'Colour: bright cherry red. Aroma: fresh raspberries and rhubarb. Palate: delicate - tastes like grapefruit, cherry, raspberries. Finish: well balanced and fresh acidity. Velvety.' Serve at 9°C.

www.jeanrivier.com

Other Argentinean producers to be aware of:

Bodegas Baldi

Www.Co-Op-2U.com sells this winery's Shiraz rosé, Mendoza region-based Bopdegas Balbi uses Malbec, Syrah and Cabernet grapes. www.bodegasbalbi.com

Chile

The history of wine in Chile began around 1550 — several decades after its discovery and conquest. Chroniclers of the period speak of the first planting of vines for the wine production immediately after Pedro de Valdivia took possession of the Chilean territory in the name of the King of Spain. As a result, Chile was more than a century ahead of South Africa in establishing its first vineyards, and became the first wine producer in the new world, some 200 years before California.

Chile may not be South America's most voluminous wine producer, but many would aver that it achieves the best quality. Its wine exports are 40-45% of overall annual production. The Chilean market has attracted investment from around the world, and accomplished wine makers have followed it there. It is now acknowledged to be on the way to parity with leading countries in terms of viti-culture and oenology. Chile's geographical traits parallel those of California, being a 'long, skinny country' defined by the Pacific Ocean and a relatively low coastal range on the west, and bigger mountain ranges to the east. Between these extremes exist conditions suitable to grow most grape varieties.

Unlike California, Chile is traversed by moderate east-west mountain ranges that create river valleys open to the Andes and to the Pacific. Land is irrigated by glacial melts from the Andes; and, in diurnal cycles, cool air blows back and forth, moderating the climate.

There are four primary wine regions within this area, which are (North to South): Aconcagua (North of Santiago, the warmest area for fine grapes), Maipo (a region where many of the major wineries are based), Rapel (a cooler region than Maipo, it includes the renowned Cochagua district), and Maule (where the Curicó district is located, cooler and less dry than Rapel; parts of this region grow Pais). The seasons are, of course, reversed from those of the Northern Hemisphere: harvest takes place mainly in March and April.

Chilean viniculture has taken time to capitalise on its centuries-old headstart, but the country's commitment to quality wines is evidenced by healthy export sales and the awarding of many prestigious international wine prizes. This expertise and attainment has spilled-over into Chile's pink wines; here is a selective survey of primary examples.

Viña Santa Rita

Although the growth of wine-making in Chile during the colonial period was slow, towards the end of the 18th Cen-

tury the first shipments of wine to other American countries left from the port of Valparaiso. Around that time, land in the Maipo Valley region that would later belong to Viña Santa Rita began to be used for grape growing.

Don Domingo Fernández, a politician, founded Viña Santa Rita in 1880 and promoted the introduction of the finest French vine stocks. Following the advice of expert French oenologists, he started producing wines using superior techniques and with superior results. Owned by successive generations of Spanish nobility, in 1980, a group of entrepreneurs acquired 50% of Viña Santa Rita, buying the remaining 50% some eight years later.

An excellent and dignified rosé comes from Viña Santa Rita — its 120 Cabernet Sauvignon Rosé (sold through Oddbins in the UK). The producer says it expects to export approximately 480,000 bottles of 120 Cabernet Sauvignon Rosé in 2003, of which 16% goes to the UK (Denmark, Canada, Holland, and Germany are the next biggest markets).

"There is a renaissance of rosé wine taking place," opines Geert-Jan van der Zanden, Commercial Manager Europe, at Santa Rita. "Ours has been doubling sales in the past two years in countries such as Holland, Denmark and Germany." van der Zanden adds: "In Holland especially, rosé has become a fashionable drink in night clubs and on beach terrasses."

The 120 Cabernet Sauvignon Rosé is made from 100% Cabernet Sauvignon grapes, and is marked by its distinctive raspberry and blackberry aromas. It will retain its quality in the bottle for up to three years.

Pellicular maceration occurs over a period not exceeding 12 hours. Fermentation is carried out at 16-18°C with selected yeast strains; the wine is matured in steel vats.
www.santarita.com
www.oddbins.com

Viña La Rosa

Viña La Rosa was founded in 1824, by Don Gregorio Ossa; the Ossa family has remained owners of the winery, but Viña La Rosa Ltd is now a subsidiary of La Rosa Sofruco SA. Viña La Rosa does two pinks — La Palma Rosé (blended from 70% Merlot and 30% Cabernet Sauvignon), and Viña La Rosa Cabernet Sauvignon-Merlot Rosé (60% Cabernet Sauvignon and 40% Merlot) — both from the Rapel region. La Palma Rosé exports to the US markets only, but Viña La Rosa is branded for the

UK as Los Rosales Cabernet Sauvignon-Merlot, and sold through Laithwaites and the Sunday Times Wine Club. In all Viña La Rosa plans to produce 18,000 cases of its rosés this year (2003), says Marine Dargery of its International Marketing department, confirming that "Rosé demand has increased".

Viña La Rosa Cabernet-Sauvignon-Merlot Rosé is harvested by machine in the third week of March. Grapes were de-stemmed, then crushed. The must is then pumped to fermentation vessels where tartaric acid is added, with a small quantity of sulphur dioxide, followed by a selected yeast culture (EC1118). The must ferments at 27°C for seven days.

The malolactic fermentation occurs naturally. The wine matures in stainless steel tanks and in bottles. Total case production was 25,000. It has an alcohol content of 13.5% vol. Tasting notes: a smooth, medium-bodied wine with herbaceous, minty aromas combined with fruit flavours of strawberries, cherries, and currants.

60 La Palma Rosé's selected grapes were hand picked in the early hours of the morning, while still very cool, to preserve the fresh fruit flavours. The must was cold macerated and fermented at a carefully controlled temperature of 14°C. Total case production of the last vintage was 20,000.

ABV is 14.5% ABV. Winemaker's tasting notes: 'Pronounced aromas of wild strawberry and hints of red cherries. On the palate, luscious notes of very ripe strawberry and hints of red apple and pear match this. Crisp acidity and a clean finish.'

www.larosa.cl
www.laithwaites.co.uk
www.sundaytimeswineclub.co.uk

Torres

Miguel Torres was an early convert to Chile's potential as a world-class wine producer. In 1979 the Spanish drinks giant was the first foreign investor in Chile (based at Curicó): growth has been prodigious: the original 100 hectares have become 330 hectares, and Torres is now a major wine presence in the area. Torres also introduced temperature-controlled stainless steel tanks and other progressive technology.

It now produces some 2m bottles a year, 70% of which are exported. The UK and Sweden are its top markets, but apparently its Santa Digna Cabernet Sauvignon Rosé is its best seller in Spain: quite an achievement in a market not exactly bereft of superb indigenous rosados. (Torres also produces its De Casta rosés using Spanish Garnacha Tinta and Cariñena grapes — the latter recuperated from old vineyards in Chile). Santa Digna's grapes are cultivated in Conca de Barberà in the heart of the Chilean Central Valley.

Its maker describes Santa Digna as a wine of distinct 'personality': original, young and nonconformist. Made from 100% Cabernet Sauvignon grapes, only a short contact is allowed between skins and juice. Santa Digna is probably the most widely-available Chilean rosé in the UK, found equally in multiples, supermarkets, onlines and bricks'n'clicks independents.

Santa Digna is an easy-drinking rosé, with fruitiness and depth, but as with any mass-produced wine it is prone to a certain sameness.

www.torreswines.com

61

Concha y Toro
Founded by Don Melchor Concha y Toro in the 19th Century, Concha Y Toro is now one of the most famous wineries in Chile, having turned itself into something of a tourist attraction, and has won many plaudits from the wine industry. It produces two pinks, Sunrise Merlot Rosé and Frontera Merlot Rosé.

www.conchaytoro.com

Other Chilean producers to be aware of

Santa Monica
Based in Rancagua, this bodega also produces 100% Cabernet Sauvignon pink — *'Color salmón, abundante aroma delicado a frutas y flores'*.

www.santamonica.cl

Los Robles
From the Curicó Valley, this winery produces Gran Roble Rosé, a 100% Cabernet Sauvignon wine.

www.losrobles.cl

Caliterra

The name derives from *la calidad de la tierra* — quality (*calidad*) and the land (*tierra*) of Chile. A partnership between the families of Robert Mondavi and Viña Errázuriz, Caliterra stems from a new generation of Chilean wineries. Robert G. Mondavi previously-of Napa Valley was among the first to recognise Chile's potential as a fine wine producing country when he visited the country in 1985. In 1991 he met Eduardo Chadwick, President of Viña Errázuriz and a descendant of Don Maximiano Errázuriz, who founded the original winery in 1870.

Created in 1996, Viña Caliterra's range of wines set out to express the quality of the fruit grown in various Chilean appellations. The valleys of Colchagua, Maipo and Casablanca were chosen for developing Caliterra's estate vineyards. In addition, close collaborative relationships were established with independent growers.

Its Caliterra Syrah Rosé is a mix of 85% Syrah, 9% Malbec, 6% Merlot, and has a 12.5% ABV content. It is sold in the UK through the Waitrose supermarket chain and other selected outlets.

Caliterra's website reports that the 2002 growing season featured an 'unusually mild winter, a cool spring and a warm, dry summer'. On March 16th, heavy rains hit part of the country, including the Colchagua Valley. Merlot and Malbec were both harvested before or shortly after the deluge, and were unaffected. Syrah ripens much later, however, and had to be carefully managed to protect the fruit.

Two winemaking techniques are used with Caliterra Syrah Rosé. One Syrah component of the blend is picked very early — at the green harvest period — to get a low alcoholic and fresh wine. This component is handpicked and whole cluster pressed. The juice is pro-tected with inert gases to avoid oxidation and the must is decanted for 48 hours. The clear must is racked off the lees, and then fermented at low temperature (15-17°C) for 30 days. The other component was sourced out of ripe grapes of Syrah, Merlot and Malbec with only one hour of skin contact.

This juice is decanted for 48 hours and then racked out of the lees and fermented at the same temperature and time. (Fermentation of one component is stopped at 10g/l of sugar to adjust blend sweetness.) The wine is then kept in contact with the lees until a month before bottling to pro-mote a 'creamy' texture.

Winemaker's tasting notes: 'Fresh, fruity, uncomplicated. Lovely pale violet-red colour. The intense aromas feature red berry fruit like strawberry, raspberry, cherries and fresh flavours like green apple and quince. The 'creamy' texture is well balanced on the palate by lively acidity, fruit flavours and a soft finish.'

www.caliterra.cl

www.waitrose.com

Chapter Six

Lebanon
&
Turkey

Wine of all grades is produced throughout the Near- and Middle East, including several ro-sés of note. Not many find their way to the UK, and then appear most often on restaurant wine lists of restaurants specialising in regional cuisine.

The focus here is on two of the most established countries producing wine of the pink style, Lebanon and Turkey. This survey is not exhaustive, and it has been impractical to include smaller wineries in both that are producing rosé of greater or lesser quantity and quality.

Determining whether the wines highlighted in this section is tricky. Often wines from these regions are imported on a relatively ad hoc basis, and although they are shipped into various European markets, they should not be re-garded as 'generally available'. As far as *Rosé Exposé* re-searchers have been able to determine, most if not all of the wines highlighted in this section are, or have been, available in the UK at some time.

Rosés are prone to slipping on and off importers' lists, so it is always best to check directly with supplier or European importer/agent if readers wish to find out if they can get hold of them. Every winery here has a website, and can take enquiries by email; many in-clude details of their importers/agents on the website it-self (though it is not always obvious where to look).

Lebanon

Lebanon's wine production is estimated at over 4m bottles a year, just over a third of which are exported, generating key revenues for this nation that, less than 15 years ago, was beset by bloody civil conflict. Before this the Lebanese wine industry had to endure the Islamic rule of the Otto-mans.

Lebanon's fertile soils were famous for their wines in an-cient times: it was shipped by the Phoenicians and rated by Rome, Greece, Athens and Carthage. At Al-Bekaa, the inland valley where most vines are grown, the environ-ment is ideal for wine production, with altitudes of 1,000 meters, rainfall average of 550mm and a summer average temperature of 25°C.

Domaine de Ksara is the oldest winery in Lebanon, founded in 1857 by Jesuit monks. It was followed in the 20th Century by Nakad (1923), Musar (1930), Kefraya (1982), Clos St. Thomas (1997), Kouroum Kefraya (1997), Wardy (1997) and most recently Massaya (1998). Many micro wineries (such as Bacchus, Domaine des Tourelles), and monasteries (Annaya), produce small volumes of wine.

Achtarout

Produces Rosée Sunset. Refreshing and vivid, this very well-balanced and generous wine, which has successfully crossed the Lebanese borders, has a 'spicy flavour' due to its vinification based on Cabernet-Franc and Syrah. Wine-maker's notes: 'It has a unique, slightly pungent aroma of red berries.'

www.achtarout.com/ksararose.htm

Château Fakra

Founded in 1985 by Dr. Carlos Guillermo Adem, Fakra's roots go back to a three-centuries-old family-owned distillery located in the heart of Mount Lebanon. The winery has recently expanded its exports worldwide. It producers two table pinks — Rosé d'Atargatis and Chateau Fakra — La Fleur — and a sweet pink aperitif/desert wine, Vin Doux Naturel. Made of 50% Cinsault and 50% Grenache, Fakra's Rosé d'Atargatis is reputed to be a complex wine, with multifarious fruity aromas, yet well-balanced and supple. La Fleur is a Grenache, Cinsault, Carignan and Syrah blend. Foodwise, good matches are scallops, marinated salmon, curried poultry. Serve at 10-12°C.

www.chateaufakra.com

68

Ksara

Ksara lies near Baalbeck, in the heart of the Bekaa — so named as it was the site of a *ksar*, or fortress, at the time of the Crusades. Ksara claims to be Lebanon's largest producer with 38% of the local market share, an average production of 1.5m bottles, of which about 40% is exported to Europe (mainly to the UK and France), North America, Brazil, and Japan.

Ksara's yearly average of 1,500 tons of grapes are not all grown on land owned by the estate — they outsource from vine growers in Mansoura, Tanail, and Kanafar. Approximately 270 hectares are planted with a wide variety of grape vines, of which the most important are Cabernet-Sauvignon, Syrah, Semillon, Grenache, Sauvignon-Blanc, Cinsault, and Merlot.

Ksara produces wines with 'strong personalities', delicate, robust, but possessed of a dry fruitiness. It has three rosés: Gris de Gris, Rosé de Ksara, and Rosé Sunset. Each is made from different grape variety combinations.

Gris de Gris is a mix of 50% Cinsault, 25% Carignan, 25% Grenache Gris grape varietals. Bleeding occurs after a short period of cold maceration. Sedimentation and fermentation are done afterwards at a temperature of 18°C. The wine is then racked-off to avoid malolactic fermentation. After being fined and stabilized by refrigeration, Gris de Gris is quickly bottled.

Winemaker's tasting notes: 'Salmon-pink, with a grey undertone, a nose of small fruits, vine flowers, peony and a touch of jasmine. Fresh and light, vivid, elegant... Can only lead to a truly cheerful palate'. Ksara also describes Gris de Gris as a 'fresh and intense... Can be drunk as a thirst quencher'. To be served chilled at 8-10°C.

Rosé de Ksara, meanwhile, is blended from 55% Cinsault, 30% Syrah, 15% Cabernet Sauvignon; bleeding occurs after a maceration of eight to 12 hours; sedimentation and fermentation take place at low temperature. At the end of the alcoholic fermentation the wine is racked-off and treated with sulphite to avoid malolactic fermentation. Winemaker's tasting notes: 'Fresh, vivid, taste of ripe fruits. Good length and suppleness on the palate with the typical light salmon pink colour of a perfectly mature Cinsault'.

Ksara's main export rosé, Rosé Sunset, meanwhile, is made out of grapes selected from the 'best vats' of Cabernet-Sauvignon (55%), Syrah (25%), and Cabernet-Franc (20%) grapes. After bleeding and 10-14 hours of maceration, fermentation is carried out at 18°C.

Once the alcoholic fermentation is completed, the wine is racked-off and sulphured to avoid malolactic fermentation. Once it has stabilised, Rosé Sunset is bottled in the spring, to preserve its ripe fruit flavours. Like its Gris de Gris, Rosé Sunset can be 'drunk as a thirst quencher', chilled at 8-10°C.

Ksara does not advise laying down: Rosé Sunset should be drunk 'before the next harvest... Why should one waste its youth?' — why indeed...

www.ksara.com.lb

Château Kefraya
Located on the steep terraces of Mount Barouk, Château Kefraya holds the second largest Lebanese local market share with 32%; Kefraya's current production of 1.5m bottles will be obsoleted by new concrete and stainless steel vats that will boost production by 500,000 bottles (the bulk for export). Its top pink is La Rosee du Château Kefraya Cinsault — quite unusual in being made from 100% Cinsault grapes.

Its winemaker's notes say that the wine 'exhales fine and tenacious fragrances with predominant notes of English sweets and red fruit... Tender and fresh on the palate, its aromas explode, revealing sweetness and floral notes that render it thirst-quenching and flattering'.

www.chateaukefraya.com

Kouroum de Kefraya
Not to be mistaken for Kefraya, Kouroum de Kefraya's estate is still young. Its two pinks are Rosé D'amour and a straightforward Rosé 2000. Both wine are blended from 70% Cinsault, 20% Grenache, and 10% Carignan. Prefermentation maceration takes 12-to-14 hours, and vinification takes s place at a temperature of 17-18°C. in double-walled stainless steel vats. To be served at 8-10°C, both wines have a 12.5% ABV. Outside of Lebanon, the wines are only available through the Washington-based importer Vins de Vie.

www.vinsdevie.com

Massaya

A new (founded 1998) estate of about 5 hectares, Massaya is actually a French-Lebanese collaboration — jointly owned by French companies Château Anjelus and Château Cheval Blanc, which both monitor the production. It exports to Europe, North America (mainly Canada), Arab countries (Dubai, Jordan, and Syria), and Japan. Massaya Classic Rosé wine uses Cabernet-Sauvignon and Syrah. www.massaya.com

Château Musar

Established in 1930 by Gaston Hochar in an 18th Century castle in Ghazir, 15 miles north of Beirut), and now run by his sons Serge and Ronald, Château Musar exports some 90% of its average annual production of 750,000 bottles. Musar can lay claim to having made a significant contribution to raising Lebanon's wine profile, having won many awards at international competitions; indeed, Musar is the first Lebanese winery to become a member of the OIV (Office International de la Vigne et du Vin). Château Musar produces no less than two pinks. First, a basic Château Musar Rosé (winemaker's notes: 'has a touch of silk with almonds'), and the Musar Cuvée Réservée. www.chateaumusar.com.lb

71

Nakad

The Nakad winery is located in the Bekaa Valley, in a town called Jdita. It was founded by Joséph Nakad, the father of four brothers, in 1923 and continues to be a family business. Nakad Winery has a total production of 700 tons a year.

The Nakad Rosé wine is made from Cinsault and Carignan, and Syrah grapes. Its winemaker's notes say it is a crisp wine, fresh and fruity. Best served at 10°C.
www.winenakad.com

Clos St. Thomas

Located in Kab Elias, where the hills of Mount Lebanon meet the plain of the Bekaa Valley, this new (ish) winery established six years ago by Said T. Touma and his family, produces 175,000 bottles, of which 80% is bound for Europe and North America. The first vintage wines were launched on the local market in December 1999. Clos St. Thomas has taken part in a lot of international fairs and has proven itself on the international market by exporting to the UK, France, Germany, Canada, Sweden, and some Arab countries.

Rosé Les Gourmets is its principal pink. Previous vintages have been made from Cinsault/Grenache/Carignan combos, but the 2002 vintage replaces the Grenache with Cabernet Sauvignon: it is 75% Cinsault, 15% Carignan, and 10% Cabernet Sauvignon.

After the grapes are stripped from their stems and crushed, this wine macerates for a short time at a temperature (16°C to 18°C). The Rosé is bottled in the spring following the harvest.

This product is the result of a combination of three different grape varieties: Cinsault gives the smoothness, Grenache gives the fruity flavour, and Carignan gives spicy and fresh taste. Best drunk within three years of bottling.

www.closstthomas.com

Domaine Wardy

Another from the Bekaa, founded in 1997, this winemaker has yet to establish a reputation; it already exports to Europe, North America, Jordan, and the Ivory Coast, with plans to start exports to Japan and Australia.

In November 1999 Domaine Wardy launched a range that includes two reds (Château les Cèdres and les Terroirs), two whites (Perle du Château and Clos Blanc), and one rosé — Rosé du Printemps.

www.domaine-wardy.com

Turkey

Turkey is the fifth-largest producer of grapes in the world, yet until fairly recently less than 3% of its vineyards yielded for wine production. This was mainly due to the alcoholic drinks ban imposed during the Ottoman reign. But with increasing 'westernisation' of its viniculture — and its tourism — Turkey's wine industry is catching up.

Good Turkish rosé — or *roze* — is scarce in the UK outside specialist suppliers to the Turkish communities. Neither are they commonly found on the wine lists of most Turkish restaurants — so do not pass up the opportunity to try if you see one.

Three big producers dominate quality Turkish wine — Diren, Doluca, and Kavaklidere — and each concern features a *roza* among their ranges.

Diren

Founder Vasfi Diren harvested his first vintage in 1958. Lökal Dry Rosé is its pink candidate. A soft-bodied dry rosé of pomegranate colour, will give a 'wholly-new dimension to your palatial pleasure when taken with various hors d'houvres, grilled fish, meals with gravy and even spiced exotic dishes', grandly say the winemaker's notes, adding it has 'special texture that is enjoyed at each and every sip'. Serve chilled to 8-9°C.

www.diren.com

73

Doluca

Doluca deploys a wide range of wines (from a wide range of grape varieties) for a Turkish producer — the majority of which, interestingly, are whites rather than reds. There are also two pinks, Villa Doluca Rosé and Doluca Rosé.

Villa Doluca Rosé from the Marmara region, near the Aegean, is made from a blend of 70% Grenache and 30% Calkarasi grapes; Calkarasi is a fruity local varietal from the Marmara region. Winemaker's tasting note: 'A rosé wine of character'. Best consumed within two years after bottle

date. Serve at 8-10°C. Doluca's entry-level pink Doluca Rosé, from Thrace on the Aagean, also comprises 70% Grenache and 30% Çalkarasi. Winemakers' tasting note: 'Fresh and fruity rosé'. Serve at 8-10°C.

www.doluca.com

Kavaklidere

Kavaklidere Wines claims to be Turkey's first and oldest private sector wine producer, established in Ankara in 1929. It produces an extensive range of wines, grapes juices, beverages and other drinks. Its two pink contenders are its Rosato — semi-sweet — and Lal — which is dry.

Made from Çalkarasi grapes (pictured) of plateau Denizli region on the Aegean, Rosato is 'a well-balanced, aromatic, and dynamic' wine, say the winemaker's tasting notes. 'Rosato... has a vivid pomegranate hue, has the aroma of red fruit, citrus fruit, and red currant'. It is best when consumed within two years of the bottling date.

74

Despite its sweetness, Kavaklidere says its Rosato is a good match with pasta, pizza, and exotic foods 'thanks to its peculiarities coming from Çalkarasi grape'. It can also be presented as an aperitif. Kavaklidere also recommends its Rosato is best when served at 4-6°C, which is fine for a pre-meal snifter but pretty chilly for a food-accompanying wine. Keeps for up to four years after bottling date.

Lal is also produced from the Çalkarasi grapes of Denizli. It is subjected to a 24-hour maceration, followed by fermentation at 18°C. Kavaklidere says that due to 'peculiarities of the soil and climate [it] observes a high natural acidity which bestows freshness' — assuming, that is, the taster equates acidity with freshness! Winemakers' tasting note: '[Has] the colour of pomegranate, the bouquet of strawberry, melon and redcurrants, and the taste has a rosehip finish' — a fruity mélange indeed. Lal is best consumed within two years of the bottling date, and is best served at 6-8°C.

Chapter Seven

Australasia & Far East

Australia

"Rosés are becoming more popular over here but it will be a long hard slog to get Aussies away from their big vanilla-y reds."
— David Ritchie, Delatite Winery

Australia and rosé wine are not closely associated. In the stereotypical 'Oz' world consisting of Bruces and Sheilas, never would a Bruce be caught drinking rosé wine. No, cobber, nothing short of 18% ABV, five-year oaked-aged red would do the job, even in 40°C; and that as a top-up to several tinnies of XXXX...

In the real world, however, there are genuine signs of a rosé renaissance down under. This was evidenced by a number of new pink wines appearing with the 2002 vintage. As the new wines attract new consumers, so the interest is being driven in a self-promotional fashion. There is even a new grape type, Malian — a 'mutation' of a Cabernet-Sauvignon — which is being targeted for rosé production, with some success.

Hard statistics are difficult to come by since Australian rosé wine production and sales data was collapsed into a 'red wine and rosé' category in 1997. Subsequently, providing straight rosé wine statistics for recent years is not straightforward.

77

Free rosé for all?
The Rosé Liberation Alliance was founded in 2000. It started as what was described as "a bit of a drinking-binge joke by a few Melbourne-based rosé lovers", but it soon built something of a following with many respected food and wine luminaries among its members, as well as several actual rosé makers. Head of the Alliance is Roy Moorfield, possibly Australia's most recognised wine expert.

Moorfield is eminently qualified to lead a rosé crusade, being blessed with the right balance of seriousness and fun: "Wine drinkers are slowly being exposed to [rosé] wines, and they love them," he told *Melbourne Age* journalist Ben Canaider in a 2001 interview.

"Over the last Christmas and New Year period I felt like a veritable John the Pink Baptist... Everywhere I went I'd take a few bottles of rosé, and force it down people's throats. When they realised they weren't drinking that sweet, bad, headache-making style of the old days, they rejoiced." However, the Rosé Liberation Alliance does seem to have gone quiet of recent — perhaps its very success has proved its own undoing, as Moorfield himself once predicted.

Aussie contenders for pink stakes

Even with the acknowledged increase in popularity, Jim McMahon, an Australia-based wine expert who tours the world lecturing on wine and giving courses, feels rosé in Australia is very much "a hit-and-miss affair" with one of the best examples in his opinion coming from Turkey Flat Vineyards, whose rosé is a blend of Grenache, Cabernet-Sauvignon, Shiraz and Dolcetto. At 12% ABV and 15.5 grams per litre of residual sugar, this is not a throwaway pink. Described as full-bodied by the winery, the Shiraz adds structure, while the Grenache adds red cherry flavours and aromas. Cabernet-Sauvignon fills the palate with raspberries whilst the Dolcetto contributes spice and freshness to this wine. The wine is available through Tanners Wine Merchants in the UK.

78 At Wirra Wirra Vineyards, grower Jonathon Hesketh explains that Australian producers use an eclectic range of grape varieties, with Grenache and the Cabernets probably used more often than others, including anything from Shiraz to Petit Verdot. More often than not, the most popular wines are not 100% dry with anything from 10g to 15g of residual sugar — but with good acidity to keep the balance, though there are always exceptions.

Wirra Wirra Vineyards bottled its first ever rosé style wine this year – Mrs Wigley (named after the cellar cat) – for sale almost exclusively on the domestic market. According to Hesketh there has been huge interest in this style from the Australian wine media, and consumer interest is also very high — after decades in the wilderness. They were surprised by selling-out of the wine after only five months on the market. Export wise, several of Wirra Wirra's foreign market trading partners are now keen to trial the rosé.

Dan Crane from Allsaints Wine gained his first experience with rosé, not in Australia, but in Bordeaux back in 1993 where he worked with the Dubourdieu family in Sauternes and Graves. The son, Denis Dubourdieu, fiercely intelligent and single-minded in his dedication to making the very best wines, told Crane of his dislike for the technique of *saignée* (or bleeding) – the most common rosé production method — as he felt it made both bad rosé and bad red – the resulting wine, in other words, once the rosé juice is run off (see tint box, page 82).

What has lasted in Crane's memory is the need to make rosés from fruit that is specific for the purpose, his current wine being made using the Merlot grape, from fruit selected specifically for rosé production.

Increasing food focus

At Geoff Merrill Wines, Scott Heidrich has been making rosé wines alongside Geoff Merrill for 10 years. Geoff, however, has been making rosé since 1977 during his time at Château Reynella, South Australia, so rosé is not a new experience at this Aussie winery. Interestingly, one of their largest selling wines in the UK market is the rosé – maybe a pointer for the future?

Given that the 'fusion' cuisine identified with Australia marries spices with herbs and fruit in a way that only rosés can easily cope with, it is not surprising to see more Aussie pinks being targeted as food wines. Murray Valley Highway has created a 2002 rosé, described as brilliantly coloured showing intense aromas of strawberry fruit freshness and hints of vanilla. It is designed to be drunk chilled *or* at room temperature, with fresh fish or spicy Thai foods or at a barbecue.

Scott Collett at Woodstock wines makes a sweet Grenache in a deep pink to red colour. Sold in a tall, clear screw capped bottle, it is aimed at the entry level red drinker, or those who enjoy big, flavoursome rosé with some sweetness.

Collett specifically notes that he has found the sweetness of a chilled rosé very soothing to put out the fire of a hot chilli dish – not uncommon in Australia. (Now who said that rosés were not food wines?)

www.geoffmerrillwines.com
www.turkeyflat.com.au
www.wirra.com.au
www.allsaintswine.com.au
www.woodstockwine.com.au
www.tanners-wines.co.uk

New Zealand

Even compared with Australia, rosé production in New Zealand is very limited, though virtually every red grape variety grown in New Zealand is used in one or other of the rosés made.

Grant Edmonds at Sileni Estates, who has been making rosés since 1990, confirmed that rosé production in New Zealand is "tiny – in the order of a few thousand cases". Merlot is the most popular grape, but Pinot Noir, Cabernet Franc, Cabernet-Sauvignon and Syrah are also used. At Sileni they work with Merlot and a little Cabernet Franc to create a dry wine, which Edmonds describes as a "serious" wine with a little more colour and body than is typical and a 14% alcohol level as a result. The wine is made by draining off some juice after a couple of days of fermentation and then matured in barrels, before being bottled with screw cap tops – very popular in this part of the world.

Edmonds notes that the wine received a five star rating from senior New Zealand wine critic, Michael Cooper. Production has doubled each year for the last three years due to local demand and the winery still sells out very quickly. Edmonds also puts the increase in popularity down to the focus on summer outdoor dining and noted that some of the most expensive restaurants are now offering good rosé by the glass. Sileni Estates now exports to South-East Asia with Europe in the plans for next year.

At Esk Valley Estate in Hawkes Bay they have been making rosé since 1991, though as senior winemaker there, Gordon Russell admits, "More for our own fun and consumption than from consumer demand". But slowly and surely they have built up a loyal following, both in restaurants and via the cellar door.

Russell is another who believes that too many people in New Zealand still associate rosé with their early wine drinking experiences – the Mateus Legacy strikes again - although many New Zealanders who have travelled around the Mediterranean have sampled European rosés and enjoyed what they tasted, to the extent that they are

The screw cap: better than corks for rosé?

"The idea that screwtops are 'common' is now old-fashioned. It's a deep perception — it hasn't got a cork, so it must be crap. But that just isn't true now."
— Anthony Worrall Thompson, Celebrity London Chef.

In Australia and in New Zealand, many winemakers are favouring the use of the Stelvin screw cap closure for rosé in preference to any form of cork. Such a radical shift must have explanation. Everyone seems to have an opinion on the subject of wine stoppers, but it is only recently that there have been any real studies done to evaluate and provide objective information on the performance of different wine bottle closures.

The Australian Wine Research Institute conducted a study where they chose a reasonably full-bodied Australian Semillon white and bottled it using 14 different closures. Their conclusion was: "The screwcap is by far the most effective seal against oxygen. If you want to prevent a wine from going brown and losing freshness, a screwcap is best".

81

The New Zealand Wine Seal Initiative has recruited 34 producers to its Wine Seal Initiative. The organisation travels to markets all round the world where New Zealand wines are sold to spread its message of screwtop superiority.

Not everyone is convinced. Of course, many wine professionals will argue that this is not applicable to all wines (and some ditto, not *any* wine), certainly not classic, slow-maturing reds or even more robust rosés designed to improve over 2-5 years. Yet properly marketed, screwtops could prove a significant value-add to rosé's fortunes by turning it into a more 'portable' tipple that would appeal to younger wine drinkers.

http://www.awri.com.au
http://www.screwcap.co.nz

now searching out local examples. The Esk Valley rosé is made from Merlot – typical of Hawkes Bay pinks – with a small amount of Malbec. It has a substantial natural alcohol level of between 12.5%-14% and is macerated for 24-36 hours before fermentation.

The flavour profile is berry fruit, and it is aimed fairly and squarely at summer "al fresco" drinking, immediately following the spring harvest, though it would last a little beyond this short period without losing character.

The Forrest Estate in Marlborough has seen a rise in the popularity of pink wines to the point where they are now exporting to several countries. The Forrest Estate rosé is a substantial (12.8% ABV) dry wine, described as a delicate rose petal red with just a hint of pink and a nose of summer strawberries and cherries, with cherries and berry fruit in the mouth.

In Central Otago at Chard Farm winery they produce a Pinot Noir rosé to give what is described as a very vibrant refreshing wine made in an off-dry style. Like most New Zealand rosés, it is produced in very limited quantities, however; and like *all* New Zealand rosés, this rarity confers a certain cachet.

82

Saignée Method – bleeding good or bad?

"When making a red wine, the wine will reflect the fruit. If something is lacking, the way to make better wine is to grow better fruit, not to discard 20%-30% of the juice to concentrate the ferment, where the likely result will be an over-extracted wine lacking palate depth. The fate of the *saignée* portion is worse, with the rosé merely a by-product of the red. The techniques used in growing fruit, harvest timing and processing would be different for the two styles if you were planning to make the best possible wines. As the 'bridesmaid', the rosé is always going to come off second best. Leaving aside the requirements of the red, the only way to make really good rosé is to let her catch the bouquet and make her the bride for a change. Fruit choice, harvesting, maceration, etc., need to be tailored to making rosé in its own right, not as a by-product."
— *Dan Crane, Allsaints Estate*

But despite small quantities still being the order of the day, it seems that, like Australia, there is a rosé renaissance of sorts happening in New Zealand. According to Peter Cunningham of Lace Fine Wine Merchants, it is no secret that the style got a bad reputation in the 1970s and 1980s through several inferior products, and is "still recovering" from this.

Cunningham believes that there are only about 20 producers currently making rosé, of which probably half a dozen could be described as 'serious', though the best examples are of very good quality, in his opinion. Even so, the larger rosé producers would still be dealing in the hundreds, rather than thousands, of cases.

It will be interesting to see just how the market develops from in future years, especially with respect to exports.

Hardcore following out of the closet?

"There seems to be a resurgence of interest in the pink drink. Hard to tell where it has come from," reckons Grant Edmonds of Sileni Estates, "but our guess is that the few local producers who have worked quietly away over the last few years making small volumes of 'serious' rosé have developed an enlightened band of followers."

Edmonds continues: "These faithful few have proved the sceptics wrong by enjoying rosé and asking for more. I've heard that a few more labels are testing the water this year, and that some retailers have actually 'come out of the closet' to stock it."

Rosé exponents are sparsely placed across the islands, and easily identifiable it seems. "I think I have the dubious title of 'Mr Rosé'," admits John Forrest, of Forrest Estate Winery in the Marlborough region of New Zealand. "This came about quite serendipitously with the making of our first rosé, and first ever wine, way back in 1990 which came about completely by accident as a result of over filling the red fermenter."

That rosé went on and won the Directors Trophy for Champion New Zealand Rosé at the Air New Zealand Wine Awards, proved to be extremely popular and as a result, they have been 'stuck' (if that is the right word) with making a rosé ever since. Over the years, their pink pro-

Hatten Wines' eastern promise

The Indonesian province of Bali has been described as "not a wine-lover's dream". The Balinese government imposes steep duties and taxes on imported wines, and itinerant imbibers can expect to be surcharged for stuff from Australasia and beyond. In any event, rosé-loving travellers are not in Bali for *vino*, but there is a home-grown wine experience that should not be missed.

Bali's grape-growing region is Singaraja, along the island's north coast. Hatten Wines launched in mid-1994, bottling a young Rosé called simply that. It later expanded to a sparkling rosé, called Jepun. Sanur-based Hatten uses a local grape Alphonse-Lavallée (pictured), known also as Ribiera seedless table grape variety (of French origin) not intended for wine and are not typically used elsewhere for that purpose. Mainstream varieties like Cabernet Sauvignon and Chardonnay were tried, but failed to fruit and were susceptible to termites.

84

The Alphonse-Lavallée is grown on overhead trellises (or *pergolas*), using small pruned trees as supporting posts. Hatten Wines' French-born winemaker Vincent Desplat makes red, white and *Méthode Champenoise* sparkling wines, plus a Pineau des Charen-

duction has steadily increased from 250 cases to 2,000 cases per vintage. Forrest's views on New Zealand rosés are not entirely encouraging, however.

"In general I feel they are a rather mixed bag. There are only a few producers who consistently make good rosés — the two that spring to my mind are Esk Valley and Te Mata. In both these cases, and indeed our own, we specifically set out to make premium rosé, have fruit in the vineyard dedicated to the task and grow and make it accordingly. "Too often it is the case here in New Zealand that rosés only appear in the bad years and are effectively failed red wines with little of the fruit, charm and vibrancy of great rosé."

However, Forrest explains that, despite this variability, the rosé segment of the market has grown and — in line tes-style apéritif. If the rest of the range is like the pinks, Desplat's is a major achievement in tropical viticulture. Hatten Rosé strikes an impressive balance between a food and drinking wine, with an alcohol content of 10.5% by volume. The bouquet has a pronounced strawberry bias, and is slightly unequal to the finesse of the taste, which is nicely balanced. The flavour is otherwise balanced and well suited to the wine's body and density. It has a clean finish that is not overlong.

Bali's tropical climate means that grapes are constantly harvested from evergreen vines every 120 days – so wine can be produced year-round. Indeed, Hatten recently celebrated its '100th vintage in seven years'.

Fermentation of Hatten's Rosé takes place in temperature-controlled stainless steel tanks, helped by selected champagne yeasts. The end result shows great integrity to the grape.

Judging by samples, Hatten Rosé is a good traveller, but unlikely to improve with age, and cellaring is not recommended. Hatten Wines is pursuing opportunities to bring its wines to the European market, and its two pinks are spearheading this; indeed they should start appearing on the wine menus of some of the UK's more upmarket Indonesian restaurants over the summer 2003. www.hattenwines.com, www.baliunkorked.co.uk

85

with other commentators – believes that it perhaps parallels the rise in New Zealand's diners move to explore culinary flavours and the bistro/outdoor café scene.

He was surprised by the ability of his wine to stand up to strong Asian cuisine such as fruit chutneys and sweet chilli dishes as well as the classic summer meat and cheese platters. But then that is what we know rosés *are* good at. According to Forrest, his rosé (available through Adnams in the UK – www.adnams.co.uk) has developed over the years to be now a reasonably consistent and equal blend of Cabernet, Merlot and Pinot Noir. The nose reflects the varietals contribution being pungent and fruity with strawberry, cherry, raspberry and redcurrant flavours. They have progressively made the wine drier each year and it is now with three to four grams per litre a very dry wine with a lovely refreshing crisp finish.

China and Japan

If you think winemaking in China – other than rice wine – is a new pursuit, then think again. Grape cultivation and wine making in China took place before the Han Dynasty, way back in 206BC. A major step forward came far more recently – in 1892 — during the last years of the Qing Dynasty when Chines Zhang Bi-shi established grape gardens and a wine company – Zhanyu Winery.

Chines Zhang Bi-shi introduced good quality grape species and machinery production methods from the West, such as replacing urns with oak barrels. China's winemaking technique stepped up to a new level. Since then, China's wine industry has gone through three stages in its development following the establishment of the People's Republic of China – the restoration at the beginning, the large-scale construction that followed and the tortuous advancement after the opening-up of the country.

But it is the success of one Mr. Guo Qi-chang's new technique in wine making in the years from 1978 to 1983 – primarily putting an end to common blending of wines and juices - which set China onto the new track of meeting required international standards.

86

The creation of the Sino-French joint venture, the Dynasty Winery Corporation, in 1980, and the birth and expansion of the Great Wall Winery, together with the old Changyu Winery, formed the triumvirate of China's wine industry as it stands today.

By the end of 1995, there were more than 240 wineries in China. With more than 100 new ones set up since 1996, the total present number is estimated at more than 300, most of them medium and small-size producers however.

Style-wise, sweet and semi-sweet wines were the mainstay before 1995, with a small amount of dry wines. However, dry wine production has shot up in recent years, with dry red leading the way, accounting for over 50% of all wine production. This includes dry rosé — there are no separate figures available. Most of the popular European grape types are grown in China, with varying degrees of success, as well as a number of indigenous varietals.

Yet another major step towards China producing true, world-quality wine has just occurred, with the arrival of official classification. It had been the norm for many producers to sell what is called 'half-juice wine'. This is created by adding sugar and water to a local grape variety (typically a wild grape called Shanputao, which literally means 'mountain grape'). The reason is that this plentiful variety never gets enough sugar to make a wine in its own right and has excessively high acid levels as a result. So, the addition of sugar and water makes it 'drinkable'.

But earlier this year, major members of the China Alcoholic Drinks Industry Association met in Beijing to discuss abandoning the so-called half-juice-wine standard and establishing a real wine classification system. It is anticipated that the half-juice wine standard will be abolished in the near future as a result. It has been recommended that all relevant wineries should start to make preparations to meet this change with a view to realising the transformation from half-juice wine to full-juice wine within six months or less.

According to Denis Gastin, an Australian wine writer who focuses on the China and Japan market, these law changes cannot come soon enough as he describes most of the pink wine produced in China as "very ordinary at best and, quite frequently, just plain horrible". However, Gastin has noted one excellent rosé from the Shanxi Province – a Cabernet Franc/Cabernet-Sauvignon/Merlot blend which, unsurprisingly, was made by a Frenchman over there in a new winery called Grace.

87

DrinkPink tasting notes: Great Wall Rosé Wine

The label, funnily enough, features a picture of part of the Great Wall of China and states the alcohol level as 11% by volume — refreshingly light to some palates – and is partially made using the Loong Yang varietal. Tasted with Chinese cuisine, in the glass it is a mid-pink, but not entirely clear. The nose is slightly sweet. In the mouth there is a general fruit flavour and a seeming complete absence of any alcohol. The kind of slight acid bite and kick that an alcoholised drink naturally gives you was completely lacking. A rosé curiosity.

www.drink-pink.com

Land of the rising rosé?

Japan may be a target market for top French, US and Australian winemakers, but it is also a wine-producing nation in its own right. In 1875, the first commercial winery was established in Katsunuma, Yamanashi, now a part of Mercian winery — the second largest wine company in Japan. However, Japan is not naturally suited to viticulture, and successful winegrowing has always been a struggle.

There are three major reasons for this. Foremost is the high humidity prevalent with plentiful rainfall during the growing season – not ideal. Second, much of the soil is very acidic. Third, there isn't actually much spare land available to plant vines on in the first place!

To help winemakers cope with the growing conditions, Japanese law states that wine can be chaptalised (i.e., sugar can be added during fermentation) and acidified. The latter is not normally required, but the Japanese do use a large amount of sugar in winemaking.

To cope with the weather, a traditional Japanese vineyard is trellised with an overhead system to avoid excess humidity from the soil and enable the vines to ripen uniformly. Through the 20th Century, many grape varieties were introduced from Europe and the US. As American varieties tended to tolerate rain and diseases, they have been increasing and cross hybrids made of American and European varieties are widespread.

Varietal experimentation

The most significant local grape is the Cosy, which has adapted well to the Japanese climate. Most Cosy wine is dry to medium, with a mid-weight and is used in white as well as rosé production. For the latter – of which very little appears to be produced – another commonly used grape variety is the Muscat Bailey A — an American hybrid typically used to produce light bodied, fruity red and rosé wines – often semi-sweet in style.

Additionally, Japanese winemakers have been experimenting with classic French varietals more recently, such as Chardonnay, Cabernet-Sauvignon, Cabernet Franc and Merlot, with a revised trellis system in place. Some successes have been noted so it will be interested to see what happens in the future; hopefully there will be something to report in the 2004 edition of *Rosé Exposé*.

But generally in Japan, rosé wine does not seem to have made its mark, either as a production wine (in what is admittedly a country with scarce repute for grape wine production) or as a popular wine for local consumption. Denis Gastin believes this is something of a paradox, as rosé wine styles are precisely what he thinks the Japanese would and should like, but they remain unpopular.

The idea of maturation of tastes is inextricably tied in with red wines. Gastin understands that a small proportion of the Japanese population has 'matured' enough to go back to the pink styles to find the serious examples, but that it is still a tiny proportion of the overall market for wine consumption.

There is at least one authentic Japanese rosé. Made by the Kizan Winery in the Kofu valley, about 90 minutes from Tokyo, the Kizan Wine Rosé is a blend of Kosyu white wine grapes and Black Queen (pictured), MBA and BBA red grape (the latter two are hybrids). Described as having a fruity flavour with light acidity, its UK availability has been unascertainable.
www.kizan.co.jp

89

Chapter Eight

Tasting rosé

Telling your pinks from your partridge eyes

*"Rosé... is a libation that varies from the palest pink to copper or
salmon, a range of colour that the French describe with a
bewildering array of names."*
— *Robin Garr, WineLoversPage.com*

Wine tasting: art, science — or pseudology?
What are the rudiments of connoisseurship?
Can anyone learn to master them — or only
bona fide wine nobs? Hearing wine authorities enthusing
over fruit 'exploding' on their palates can leave an overrid-
ing impression of plums in the mouth: to many, wine tasting argot is synonymous with posh gab, despite attempts
to colloquialise it in recent years.

But an ability to analyse and assess a wine by tasting is no
longer deemed the preserve of sommeliers and Masters of
Wine; there are many professional and semi-professional
tasters with no formal qualifications. Some famous wine
critics and authors have gained tasting skills inciden-
tally, by rote.

93

So how good a taster can the average wine drinker
become? How good a taster do they *need* to be?

The *Rosé Exposé* Four Fruits Scale puts the case for a
more focused method specifically for tasting rosé wines. It
proposes that rosés can be simply identified and appreciated using a simple codification based on fruitiness zones.

Wine tasting jargon busting

There is plenty of no-nonsense tasting guidance to be found in wine books and wine websites, but despite its sensory nature, it remains pretty cerebral. The ability to taste wine 'properly' — in accordance with preordained methods and criteria — invokes a language of adepts and savants, without which wine cannot be 'properly' enjoyed.

Many newspapers and magazines have wine columns, and their styles borrow from the purple prose of traditional 'wine lit'. Wine writing of this genre can incline toward familiar turns of phrase and imagery. Given the demands made on wine journalists to come up with differential terms for each wine they cover, this is bound to happen. Using clichés to describe wines that are clichéd in style is sometimes inevitable.

Anyone who drinks wine over a period of time learns more about it (and its effects), and starts articulating their impressions. Wine drinkers cannot help but express their pleasure — and displeasure — to anyone ready to listen; we are all, to an degree, tasters manqué.

94 That's no bad thing. Tasting terminology serves a purpose. It enables articulation of subjective reactions to a unique experience. It also enables the differences between wines to be compared and codified so that their attributes are understood by everyone involved.

The tenets of tasting — acidity, aroma, balance, bouquet, depth, length, dryness, sweetness, etc. — are the argot of the wine world. And as with any other language, the more you master it, the more readily it trips off the tongue.

Jargon as a purchasing aid

Wine fanciers do need to understand the jargon to make informed buying decisions. On a more commercial note, wine tasting needs to serve winemakers and wine sellers by encouraging people to buy the wines that are under consideration.

Jargon need not be the same as 'Winespeak' — classifying wines in terms of analogical comparisons and similes. This often invites – and receives – ridicule. Likening a wine's bouquet to an old leather saddle, scorched daffodils, briar chips, mouldy seed cake or mulled cat's pee, becomes all the more risible where it is taken half-seriously.

A taste for tasting

With top tasters much skill is hardwired into their olfactory and gustatory systems, and developed and refined by dint of long experience. The abilities to appraise wines visually also come with time. There is no fast-track to such expertise.

Less accomplished tasters show a bias on either side of the nature/nurture divide. Tasters working at the sharp end of the market need to add speed to their skillset, often having to appraise dozens of wines in a single day. Tasters are mostly passionate about wine, and also about their view of what makes a wine worthy of praise.

In this respect they vary greatly: some will bang-on about *terroir* and minerality; others about grape varietals and blend percentages; production methods are a perpetual stalk of contention. Such tasters are adamant in their convictions, and will brook no contrary views. Wine bigots abound, and in provoking opinion play a useful role.

Budding connoisseurs are faced with a more practical question: if they feel unsure about their ability to detect evidences of good and not-so-good wine, does this invalidate their enjoyment of it, or indeed of the merits of the wine tasted? Can a poor wine be 'redeemed' if people do nonetheless enjoy it?

This question has special resonance to rosé: because of the way it is made, pink wines' properties are commonly not as pronounced as those of red and white. This has played a part in rosé's underestimation; it also means that its fans need to adopt a different sensorial approach to tasting rosé.

Vocabulary of tasting

Rosé is described as pink wine, but it comes in many colours that seem far removed from things pink: *vin gris* (gray wine), to *oeil de perdrix* (partridge eye), to *pelure d'oignon* (onion skin), for example. But the most popular descriptive terms compare these wines taste and colour in terms of fruit and flora, particularly the former. All wines may be described as fruity to degrees, but this approach is highly relevant to rosé, as pink wine generally has a narrower taste range than red or white: the processes that determine degrees of taste and texture are much reduced in the production of rosé.

The grape compounds are fresher, and its juice does not have the same exposure to skins and must. The maceration and fermentation periods are shorter; it is less exposed to stabilising additives that may (or may not) affect taste, and little rosé is stored in wooden casks that will impart 'oakiness'. And because it is imputed that rosés should be drunk young, they are largely consumed before they have had a chance to acquire additional levels of characteristics through maturation.

In view of these innate differences, it seems odd that rosés are tasted and assessed in the same way as reds and whites — but they are. Rosé is just as capable of delivering as complex a tasting experience as whites and reds from the same vineyard, but it seems obvious that different tasting criteria be applied.

Four Fruits Scale

The *Rosé Exposé* Four Fruits Scale creates a framework for appreciating rosé from a customised angle. It is a tasting guide that can help rosé fans devise a simple way of differentiating pink wines. It makes describing pink wines simple and easy to remember. It is not a rigid idea; use the Four Fruits Scale as much or as little as you need.

Winesellers often provide an indication of how dry or sweet a wine is. Dryness is a such common characteristic of rosés, that medium and sweet pinks of commensurate quality are unusual (in the UK at least). The Four Fruits Scale is designed just to gauge taste, smell and colour properties. It draws on terms of reference that are already commonly found when assessing rosé wine, when appraisers cite the same bunch of fruits again and again.

These range in flavour intensity typically from the concentrated fruitiness of red cherry (*prunus*), through to strawberry (*fragaria*) and raspberries (*rubus*), to the paler, more acerbic taste ranges found in pink grapefruit (*citrus paradisi*). The table opposite divides them into zones.

Because rosé is deemed a 'summertime' tipple, its characteristics are usually compared to summer fruits, although the Four Fruits Scale extends this calendar link to include fruits that appear in other seasons. But that many rosés are largely redolent of ripe strawberries and raspberries happens to be true, even though these do not have much in common with grapes. Paradoxically, rosés can show the taste and colour qualities of strawberry, with an absolutely citrusy bouquet.

The variations between these groups represent a spectrum of colours, flavours, smells, and viscosities, which are capable of being both contrasting and complementary. Roughly speaking, this spectrum reflects the same diversity of rosé types: the fuller-bodied pink wines made with a high percentage of grapes that can cope with extended maceration will have distinctive cherry/strawberry noses, while those allowed a briefer exposure to the skins (etc.) will have less strident hue and bouquet.

Rosés certainly show general regional characteristics. Those of Côtes de Provence, for instance, tend to be lighter and more 'delicate' than those from other parts of France — but light, delicate rosés will also come from Bordeaux, Loire, Gaillac, and the Languedoc. But their shared

Zone 1	Zone 2
Red cherry	*Strawberry*
Alkalinity: pronounced	**Alkalinity:** medium
Acidity: light	**Acidity:** medium-variable
Body: full	**Body: light**-medium
Fragrance: pronounced	**Fragrance:** medium-pronounced
Zone 3	Zone 4
Raspberry	*Pink grapefruit*
Alkalinity: intermediate	**Alkalinity:** light
Acidity: light-variable	**Acidity:** pronounced
Body: Medium-full	**Body:** light
Fragrance: intermediate	**Fragrance:** light

stylistic qualities are a better key to understanding how they will show on the palate and the nose. As well as representing a spectrum of taste component grades — fruitiness, sweetness/dryness, alkalinity/acidity, body density, and so on, the Four Fruits Scale provides a concomitant gauge of aroma intensity and colour depth that can be reasonably ascribed to these properties in a rosé wine. What kind of body colour does the liquid have? Deep ruby, like a Spanish rosado, or less opaque, like a Provence rosé? Has the aroma the broad, pungent fruitiness of a Cabernet-Sauvignon or Syrah-based rosé, redolent of ripe strawberries? Or does it possess the sharp citrusy tangs of a wine bled from Cinsault or Grenache skins? The Four Fruits Scale gives you an olfactory/degustatory map by which to place a given rosé's sensorial qualities.

How to use it

When tasting a rosé, see which of the fruit zones you feel it resembles most in flavour and fragrance. It might take several sniffs and sips to place it satisfactorily. You can then rate the degree of resemblance on a point scale of one-to-five (or one-to-ten if you feel your sensitivity is more acute).

Using a pre-printed taster's book or just an ordinary notebook, keep a note of your impressions, using the Four Fruits Scale matrix as a shorthand *aide-de-memoir*; don't forget to append your general reactions to the wine – did you like it? Would you recommend it to yourself again? How better/worse did it compare to other rosés of recent memory? If consumed with a meal, how well did it complement the cuisine? How much did it cost, and was it well priced?

It is likely that your impression of a rosé straddles two or even three of the fruit zones — in the case of a medium rosé wine typical of a Bordeaux or hearty pink from the Loire, you could rate it... *Zone 1 (red cherry) x2, Zone 2 (strawberry) x1, Zone 3 (raspberry) x2.*

A lighter rosé, from Côtes de Provence such as the Château Moutète pictured on page iii of the colour pages section, maybe, or a Listel Gris, might rate *Zone 2x1, Zone 3x2, Zone 4x4.*

Because rosés are frequently drunk young before they have had a chance to become robust, they can seem possessed of contrasting flavours and bouquets. Even pinks made from single grape varietals such as Syrah or Merlot seem lively and less rarefied than equivalent reds and whites.

Many contemporary winemakers like to experiment with the grape constituency of their rosés — some will blend as many as five different varietals in a single vintage. And this is no modern experimentation methodology applied solely to low-end rosés. Even classics such as Tavel can be found to contain multiple grape varieties. Some rosé buffs aver that it is this scope for intricate, delicate concoction that imbues rosé with its special appeal.

An interest in trying different blend combinations is one of the signs of the new generation of quality rosés, so be sure to check the label, usually the rear label, for data about this.

A knowledge of single-varietal rosés will naturally inform appreciation of the blends where the same varietals are used. Over time, rosé buffs, like all wine buffs, start to discern which varietals they like best, and in which combinations (if any).

99

Wine appreciation is as much about finding your own taste in wine and realising that you are not obliged to bow to the consensus. It is OK to dislike even the finest wines, and that applies just as much to fine rosés as any other colour of wine. There is bad *fine* wine too.

The Four Fruits Scale enables rosé aficionados to get a general sense of the different styles of pink wines, and build-up a profile of the kinds of rosé they prefer, and therefore like to try in the future.

Wine writers like to exhort consumers not to return to wines that they know and like, and urge them to be 'adventurous' and 'experiment' in their choices. It seems that most people who drink wine on a regular basis do commonly stay with what they know and like, and will only try new wines if they are known to bear similarities with their favourites. The Four Fruits Scale gives them their 'stick in the ground' by which to compare and contrast wines, so they can experiment with more assured confidence in their selections.

Chapter Nine

Rosé
and
cuisine

Matching pink wine with food

"I can drink Provençal rosé till the bourride is cooked and way beyond the aioli" – Keith Floyd, *Floyd Uncorked.*

Along with being underrated as superb wines in their own right, rosés have constantly been overlooked as the ideal accompaniment to good food. Countless wine guides proffer pages of suggestions for matching wine with cuisine; yet it is rare to find a rosé included, unless it is as an aperitif or maybe a dessert wine.

This Anglo-Saxon take on wine and food pairing is contradicted by the canon of cuisine from rosé-producing regions, where rosé is paired with food as customarily as whites or reds are. Some of these traditional pairings are explored below.

There are many foods for which rosé is the perfect partner. Broad characteristics, such as rosé's fruitiness, can invigorate dry foods with low-key flavours — poultry such as turkey, or root vegetables. They are good with salads — especially meated salads — where a white wine may overwhelm light, green leaf collations. They work just as well with fruited salads.

Rosés go best with pink-coloured comestibles — from salmon to grapefruit, rosé is often a better pairing than white. Many top chefs and cookery experts stipulate rosé as the best accompaniment to many creations inspired by the Mediterranean culinary traditions. Pairing a rosé with a prawn or veal dish would not cause a second thought on the part of a French or Spanish gourmet.

The custom is less prevalent in other rosé-producing regions, but it is there — even in the US. Alas, it is mainly in the UK that anti-rosé movement seems to be in force. Got any favourite recipes or food-pairing suggestions with a rosé bias? Email info@rose-expose.com — we may be able to include them in future editions. Over the following pages we present a range of rosé-ready recipes that unite a range of different rose styles with a diversity of cuisines to create multi-course meals, starting with a rough guide to pairing pink wines and meal types.

103

Salads

In the South of France, rosés are famously associated with salads, especially salad niçoise — the Côte d'Azur equivalent of 'pie and a pint' (well, perhaps not). A classic niçoise comprises (fresh) flaked tuna with hard-boiled egg, green beans and black olives, draped in anchovies, with an olive oil dressing. However, this template is not always followed to the book in many restaurants, with green leaves, tomatoes, cucumbers and red/green/yellow peppers added willy-nilly, according to the whims of the chef/kitchen staff. So if your French permits, niçoise purists should always check on the constituents before ordering. Also ensure that the arrival of the bread basket coincides with the salad itself — it's essential to add substance to the starter.

But rosé also works well with most salads, particularly those with a higher meat, seafood or citrus fruit component (see Fruits/desserts below).

Fish

Although most gastronomes routinely recommend white wine for fish dishes, there's a lobby of opinion that would insist that for some kinds of fish, rosé is the better

choice — particularly pink fish such as salmon and trout and meatier species like tuna, swordfish, and marlin. Whether rosé is right for oily fish, like mackerel and herring is a moot point — which is no reason not to give it a try. How the fish is prepared has a bearing on its compatibility, as rosé tends not to pair well with fried foods.

Certainly pink wine is recommended for sardines in Greek cuisine, and in grilled and baked fish dishes from all around the Mediterranean, but even less-characterful rosés are apt to overwhelm smaller white fish, and do not make good accompaniments to flaky white fish.

Some gastronomes propose rosé as a good accompaniment to fresh water fish like carp and pike with 'smoky' flavours — though this is much a matter of personal taste, and will depend on how the fish has been seasoned.

Chefs also commend rosé as an accompaniment to fish stews like *bouillabaisse* (a rich fish casserole) and *bourride* (a garlic-sauced seafood stew) — though eaten in the cool of the evening, rather than as a lunchtime repast on a blazing hot afternoon...

Shellfish
Rosé works as well with pink shellfish, as it does with pink fish. The piquancy of prawns, crevettes and shrimps combine deliciously with rosés, particularly when they form the basis of a *salade aux fruits de mer*. Other shellfish, such as mussels, oysters, squid and octopus are traditionally served with specialist white wines, but a crisp pink, edging towards the white end of the taste spectrum works equally well, especially with *moules marinières*. For Spanish classics like a paella — with shrimp, clams, and scallops — what better than a robust rioja rosado?

Poultry
Arguably, rosé is a better complement for dryer white birds, such as turkey, but not chicken, capon or poussin. An exception here is chicken provençal, where a predominantly tomato-based sauce would be incompatible with a white wine, yet submerged by a red. Chicken served with bacon can also benefit from a rosé accompaniment. Rosé can even be drunk with smaller paler game such as guinea fowl, quail, or even pheasant and pigeon.

Red animal meat
One notable exception to the red meat/red wine convention is back bacon, which, either served on its own, or diced into casseroles or other dishes (such as chicken — see above), blends well with rosé.

White animal meat
Rosé can accompany white meats, though is probably not at its best except with veal (especially with fuller-bodied, Mourvèdre-based rosés, like those from Bandol).

Pasta
Pasta dishes where sauces do not predominate make ideal table fellows for rosatos from mainland Italy, Sicily and Sardinia. Examples of this are dishes like penne siciliana, where the pasta is melded with a dense tomato sauce full of vegetables and white beans.

Fruits / desserts
Rosé is frequently recommended as a dessert wine, and although it is not — strictly speaking — a 'true' dessert wine like a muscat or marsala, it sits well with sweeter courses, and desserts with fresh fruit elements — particularly citruses: oranges, tangerines, grapefruits. Sorbets also combine well with rosés.

Wine: dry Loire rosé — e.g. a Sancerre

Salad of duck fillet with pears

Preparation time: 50 min
Cooking time: 10 min

Ingredients for 4

1 washed and peeled carrot
1 washed celery stalk

} cut into matchstick lengths of about 1¾" (4cm)

A few leaves of thoroughly
    washed water cress (or lambs lettuce)
2 green conference pears
3 ½ oz (100g) pine kernels or crushed walnuts
2 duck breasts
Vinaigrette made with salt and pepper and
2 tbsps (30ml) sherry or cider vinegar
6 tbsps (90ml) walnut oil

Method

1.   Plunge the carrot and celery matchsticks into boiling salted water. Bring to the boil once more then imme-diately, carefully drain and reserve the vegetables for later.

106

2.   Simmer the orange zest in a small amount of water for 1 minute. Drain and dry carefully.

3.   Fry the duck breasts, first skin-side down, then turn. Finish skin-side down, in a pre-heated pan without additional fat or oil, for a total of 3 to 4 min-utes per side. The duck breasts should remain pink inside. Allow to cool completely.

4.   Peel and core the pears then cut into fine strips. Add the pine kernels (or walnuts) to 2/3 of the vinaigrette then mix gently with the pears. Arrange the mixture on 4 plates and sprinkle with the carrot and celery sticks.

5.   Once the duck breasts have cooled, cut into fine strips and brush with the remaining vinaigrette.

6.   Arrange the duck strips over the pears alternated with the cress leaves. Decorate with the orange zest and serve immediately.

Wine: Côtes du Frontonnais (or Comté Tolosan) rosé

Asparagus with wild mushrooms and smoked bacon
Preparation time: 50 min
Cooking time: 25 min

Ingredients for 4 as a starter

16 large white asparagus peeled and washed thoroughly
4 thick slices of smoked streaky bacon cut into thin strips
7 oz (200g) of fresh morels (or other similar wild mushrooms – small oyster mushrooms will suffice)
3 ½ oz (100g) butter
Juice of half a lemon
2 shallots
4 fl. oz (100ml) poultry stock
2 tbsps of chopped chives
salt and pepper

Method

1.   Plunge the asparagus into a large pan of boiling water, covering them completely. Bring back to the boil and boil briskly for 7 minutes. When the asparagus are cooked but still firm, drain and run under cold water to cool then drain again. Cut the base of the asparagus to ensure they are of equal length. Reserve.

107

2.   Put the bacon strips in a pan, covered with cold water. Bring slowly to the boil. Drain, run under cold water, drain again and reserve.

3.   Cut-off the earthy base of the stalks of the wild mushrooms then run under cold water to ensure that any dirt is removed. Drain and dry very thoroughly in a clean cloth.

4.   Season the boiled asparagus with salt and pepper. In a large frying pan, melt 1¼ oz (40g) of the butter and gently fry the asparagus until coloured on all sides. Arrange on 4 serving plates and pour over the squeezed lemon juice. Keep warm.

5.   Peel and finely chop the shallots. Using the same pan as for the asparagus, melt 1½ oz (40g) of butter, then

fry the bacon strips until well coloured. Drain on absorbent kitchen paper. Still in the same pan, fry the mushrooms over a high heat for 2 minutes, stirring frequently. Add the chopped shallots, poultry stock and the bacon strips and cook over a medium heat for 3 minutes. Remove from the heat, add the remaining butter and the chopped chives and mix gently.

6. Pour the bacon strip and morel mixture over the asparagus and serve immediately.

~~~~~~

NOTES

Côteaux du Languedoc rosé

Red Mullet Tartlets with spicy leek and tomato

Preparation time: 30 mins
Cooking time: 30 mins

Special equipment: 8 individual fluted tartlet tins about
4" (10cm) diameter

Ingredients for 8 as a starter

1 lb (500g) Red mullet fillets (2 medium or 3 small per
person)
1 leek
1 tbsp olive oil
½ - 1 medium tin of chopped tomatoes
1 tsp Chinese chilli and garlic mix OR & clove garlic,
chopped and ½ green chilli, chopped
a little extra olive oil
salt and pepper to taste

For the pastry:
8 oz (225g) plain flour
4 oz (110g) vegetable margarine
½ tsp salt
1 egg, beaten
1 tsp lemon juice.

2 tbsp walnut oil
½ tsp mild French mustard
1 tbsp balsamic vinegar
salt and pepper to taste
Mixed salad leaves (preferably including radicchio, frisée
lettuce and rocket)

Method
1. Pre-heat the oven to 425°F, 210°C, gas mark 6.
2. SHORT CRUST PASTRY: sieve the flour with the salt,
    then rub the margarine into the flour until the mix-
    ture resembles fine breadcrumbs, mix in beaten egg
    and lemon juice and combine to form a firm dough.
    Leave to rest.
3. Cut of the ends of the leek then cut in half lengthwise.
    Clean carefully to remove any dirt or grit then slice

into very thin semi-circles.

4. Gently heat the olive oil in a small frying pan and add the leeks, frying gently until softened. Add the chilli and garlic mix or chopped garlic and chilli and fry briefly. Add the chopped tomatoes, cover with a lid and cook steadily until well reduced (about 20 minutes).

5. While the leek and tomatoes are cooking, roll out the pastry very thinly and use to fill the 8 greased tartlet tins. Bake these blind (using pieces of aluminium foil and baking beans to keep the pastry flat) towards the top of the oven for 10 minutes.

6. The above steps can be carried out in advance.

7. Fill the part-cooked pastry cases with the leek and tomato mixture then arrange the red mullet fillets on top. Drizzle with a little olive oil, season with freshly milled salt and pepper and cook for 10 to 15 minutes.

1. While the tartlets are cooking combine the salad dressing ingredients and mix with the salad leaves. Arrange the salad leaves around the edge of 8 plates. When the tartlets are cooked, un-mould and serve in the centre of the salad.

~~~~~~

NOTES

Wine: Marsannay or Tavel rosé

Smoked bacon Gougères

Preparation time: 40 min   Cooking time: 30 min

Ingredients for 4

4 oz (100g) of smoked streaky bacon
scant ½ oz (10g) butter
scant 2 oz (50g) Comté cheese if you can get it (or strong
Cheddar, if not)
salt and pepper
Choux pastry:
12 fl. oz (350 ml) water
5 ½ oz (165g) butter
½ tsp (2½ ml) salt
½ tsp (2½ ml) sugar
8 oz plain flour, sieved
6-7 eggs

Method

1. Cut the bacon into thin strips. If the bacon is
    very salty, first place in a pan with cold water,
    bring to the boil and simmer for 5 or 6 minutes,
    drain, rise in cold running water and drain
    again. Fry the bacon strips in the butter until
    lightly browned. Reserve.
2. Cut the cheese into 40 fine slices.
3. CHOUX PASTRY: Pre-heat the oven to 350°F (180°C,
    gas 4). Put the water, butter, salt and sugar in a large
    pan and bring to the boil. Remove from the heat and
    pour in the flour in one go and beat swiftly with a
    wooden spoon to obtain a smooth dough as quickly as
    possible. Replace on the heat and continue to beat the
    dough briskly for 4 to 5 minutes until the dough
    leaves the sides of the pan. The dough should now be
    sufficiently dried. Remove the pan from the heat and
    beat in the eggs one at a time until they are
    completely absorbed, add only sufficient eggs so that
    the dough still holds its shape and is not too wet.
4. As soon as the dough is finished add the bacon strips.
    Cover a baking sheet with non-stick baking parch-
    ment. Using a piping bag with a large nozzle pipe 40
    small balls onto the sheet. Place a strip of cheese onto
    each ball. Bake in the oven for 20 minutes.
    Serve immediately.

Wine: Cabernet d'Anjou rosé

Apple, peach and nectarine Tarte Tartin

Preparation time: 1 hour 10 min
Cooking time: 25 min
Equipment: 8" (20cm) cake tin or 4 smaller (3-4") deepish
tart moulds, non-stick

Ingredients for 4

4 oz (110 g) sugar
3 ½ fl. oz apricot pulp
4 ripe peaches
2 ripe nectarines
2 golden delicious apples (or other sweet eating apple)
2 oz (50g) butter
2 oz (50g) flaked almonds
8 oz (200g) rolled out thinly into an 8" (20 cm) circle of
puff pastry (or 4 smaller circles)

Method

1. Put 1oz (30g) of sugar and 1 tablespoon of water
    into a thick based saucepan. Bring to the boil and
    allow to cook over a high heat until golden. Remove
    from the heat and mix in the apricot pulp. Chill for at
    least an hour.

2. Pre-heat the oven to 350°F (180°C, gas 4). Remove
    the peach and nectarine skins by plunging into boil-
    ing water for 30 seconds. Remove the stone and cut
    each into 8 segments. Peel and core the apples and
    cut into 8 segments.

3. Put 3oz (80g) of sugar, the butter and 2 tablespoons
    of water in small thick based saucepan. Bring to the
    boil, then allow to cook over a high heat to obtain a
    brown caramel. Immediately pour the caramel into
    the cake tin or 4 smaller tart moulds. Spread in the
    almonds then arrange the fruit segments. Cover the
    tart(s) with the puff pastry and bake for 20 to 25 min-
    utes for the large tart and about 15 minutes for the
    small tarts.

4. Invert the tart (or tarts). Cut the large tart into 4 por-
    tions. Serve with the chilled apricot caramel and
    home-made vanilla ice cream.

Wine: Touraine-Amboise rosé sec

Pan-fried scallops with ratatouille-filled Yorkshire puddings
Preparation time: 1 hour
Cooking time: 30 mins
Special equipment: Baking tray for individual cakes or muffins (about 3", 7-8cm in diameter)

Ingredients for 4

4-6 scallops per person (depending on size)
½ glass of white wine
Marinade for the scallops:
1 tbsp olive oil
1 tbsp light soy sauce
1 large clove of garlic, crushed
A squeeze of fresh lime juice
1 tbsp of gin (or sake)
A few twists of Szechuan Pepper (available from most Chinese supermarkets)

For the Ratatouille:
2 courgettes cut into small dice
1 small aubergine cut into small dice
½ each of medium-sized red and green peppers, cut into small squares
2 fresh tomatoes (or tinned equivalent) skinned after immersing for 30 seconds in boiling water, finely chopped
1 onion finely chopped
1 large clove of garlic crushed
1 tbsp olive oil
1 glass of dry rosé wine
1 dessert sp of red pesto or sprig of fresh basil, chopped
Pinch of oregano (or marjoram)
Salt
Black pepper

For the Yorkshire puds:
3 oz (85g) plain flour sieved
1 large egg
3 ½ fl oz (100 ml) milk
1½ fl oz (45 ml) water
½ tbsp freshly chopped mixed herbs (or ½ tsp dried)

113

Method

1.   1 hour before cooking commences. Combine the ingredients for the scallop marinade in a shallow dish. Rinse the scallops (leave them intact with the corals on) in cold water, drain, dry, then add to the marinade, turning them to cover all sides.

2.   PUDDING BATTER: (this can be done several hours in advance). Combine the milk and water in a jug. Whisk eggs in a suitable bowl then gradually combine the plain flour and milk and water with the eggs, adding a little of each at a time and whisking thoroughly to ensure a lump-free batter.

3.   Prepare ingredients for the ratatouille.

4.   10 minutes after you have started marinating the scallops pre-heat the oven to 400°F, 200°C, gas mark 6. After 10 minutes put in the baking tray to pre-heat with a drop of olive oil in each mould.

5.   RATATOUILLE: (can also be prepared well in advance and does improve in flavour over a 24 hour period). Heat olive oil in a medium-sized (wide rather than tall) non-stick pan or Le Creuset style pan, and when hot – but not smoking – add the onions and turn the heat down. Stir, so as not to let them stick – you don't want to brown them – for a minute, then add the aubergine and courgettes. Continue stirring for two minutes, then add the crushed garlic and the peppers. Stir round for a minute. Add the chopped tomatoes and the pesto (or basil) and the oregano. Stir round again. Add the glass of rosé wine, season to taste and cover the pan. Cook on a gentle light for 10 minutes, stirring from time to time. At this point the vegetables should be softened but not mushy. Turn off the heat and leave the ratatouille to stand.

6.   YORKSHIRE PUDDINGS: after pre-heating the baking tray with oil for 10 minutes, keep the baking tray hot on top of the stove, give the batter a stir then pour into the moulds. Put immediately into the oven at medium height and cook for about 30 minutes until golden brown and crispy.

7.   SCALLOPS: Just before the puddings are done, drain

the scallops and reserve the marinade liquid. Heat a table-spoon of olive oil in a non-stick frying pan. When hot, but not smoking, add the scallops, and turn the heat down to medium. After a minute, shake the scallops to turn them and fry for another minute. Now add in the leftover marinade and the white wine, cover the pan and cook for an extra minute.

8.   Meantime, place a single pudding in the centre of a heated plate, and fill with the ratatouille mixture, leaving as much juice as possible in the ratatouille pan.

9.   Now add the scallops, evenly spaced, in a circle around the puddings. Strain the ratatouille sauce into the remaining juice in the scallop pan, quickly reheat and pour in a circle covering the scallops and serve.

~~~~~~

NOTES

Wine: full-bodied Languedoc or Rhone rosé

Chicken breasts in pesto, coriander and tequila with wild mushroom noodles and slices of courgette and pepper

Preparation time: 30 mins
Cooking time: 20 mins

Ingredients for 4

4 free-range chicken breasts, skinned (you can also use turkey escalopes, guinea fowl or pheasant breasts for this dish – note that turkey escalopes require a shorter cooking time)

For the chicken:
1 tbsp olive oil
Sufficient red or green pesto to cover one side of each chicken breast
1 tbsp light soy sauce
1 large clove of garlic, crushed
1 tbsp of coriander seeds
Freshly ground black pepper
1 small glass of tequila
1 small glass of white wine
1 ladle of chicken stock
1 large fresh tomato, peeled and chopped.

For the noodles:
Try to buy authentic Chinese noodles from a Chinese supermarket, as they are far better than the mass-produced version commonly available in high street supermarkets. They are sold in packs containing little bundles of noodles. Allow one bundle (approx. 2 oz) per person.
8 oz of mixed wild mushrooms – e.g., shitake, oyster.

A combination of fresh mushrooms and dried (again available in Chinese supermarkets or French / Italian specialist shops) can be used. Follow the instructions on the packet for the dried mushrooms.
1 tbsp butter and/or olive oil

For the vegetables:
2 large courgettes, cut into thirds, length-ways, then each

'third' cut into three slices, length-ways. Reserve 16 pieces for cooking.

1 large green pepper cut into eight flat pieces

1 large red (or orange) pepper cut into eight flat pieces

1 tbsp light soy sauce

1 tbsp groundnut oil

1 tsp honey

1 large clove of garlic (crushed)

Dash of chilli sauce (optional)

Method

1. VEGETABLES: Pre-heat the oven to 400°F, 200°C, gas mark 6 for 15 minutes.

2. Skin the peppers by placing the cut pieces, skin-side up, under a hot grill until the skin bubbles and starts to peel. Remove and peel off the skins. In a large oven-proof dish (e.g. a large lasagne dish), combine the soy sauce, olive oil, honey, garlic and (optional) chilli and mix well. Now add the pieces of courgette and peppers, and turn them in the mixture until they are well coated by it. Then lay them out in the dish so that they are in a single layer (if neces-sary use two dishes).

117

3. Place the dish of peppers and courgettes into the oven and cook for 15 minutes, or until softened and slightly seared at the edges, but not brown.

4. MUSHROOM MIXTURE : Gently melt the butter and olive oil in a large, deep, non-stick frying pan, add the chopped mushrooms, turn so that they are all coated in the butter/oil mixture and fry gently for five minutes, stirring/tossing regularly, until they are gen-tly browned. Add a dash of soy sauce and continue to brown for two minutes, adding pepper to taste.

5. CHICKEN: Heat up a non-stick pan and, when hot, add the coriander seeds and dry-fry for a minute, shaking the pan from time to time. Crush the seeds using a pestle and mortar.

6. In a large frying pan, heat the olive oil and gently cook the crushed garlic for a few seconds, making sure it doesn't brown. Add the chicken breasts, press-ing the garlic into the breasts. Now spread a layer of pesto on the top side of each chicken breast, then turn

the breasts over, pesto-side down and cook for two
minutes on a medium heat. The pesto should form a
kind of crust.

7.   Meantime, sprinkle some soy onto what is now the
top side of the breasts and add the crushed coriander
seeds, a twist of black pepper and press this into the
top side of the breasts. Now turn them back over and
cook for another two minutes. Mix together the tequila and wine, then add to the chicken. Cook for two
minutes, so that the juice is boiling and reducing,
then add the chicken stock, cover the pan and cook
for two more minutes, or until the chicken is just
cooked (test with a skewer inserted into the middle of
each piece — the juices should run clear).

8.   Remove the chicken from the pan and keep warm.
Now add the chopped tomato to the sauce and cook
over a high heat for one minute to reduce the sauce
by about half. Now add in a tablespoon of crème
fraîche, mix well, then turn off the heat, covering with
a lid to keep warm.

9.   NOODLES: Follow the instructions on the
packet for the noodles. Typically you have to soak
them in cold water for a couple of minutes, then boil
them for 2-3 minutes. Drain and stir into the mushroom mixture

10.   Serve the noodles in a crescent shape on the plate. Arrange alternate pieces of courgettes and peppers
around the rest of the edge of the plate to complete a
circle. Then place a chicken breast in the middle of
each plate and cover with the sauce. Add a pinch of
finely-chopped fresh parsley on top and serve immediately.

Chapter Ten

Buying rosé

Reaping the rosé
retail revolution

There has never been a better time to buy rosé in the UK (or anywhere else, come to that). UK winesellers add more pinks to their lists each year and, despite the best efforts of the Treasury, rosé prices represent excellent value for money – particularly compared to the whites and reds you will get for the same price. Internet wine shops are making dozens of rosés available to UK buyers for the first time, adding yet more options for the buyer.

Whether you are buying to extend your wine knowledge, to furnish your wine cellar, or to drink straight away, here are a few pointers for buying online, as well as direct from producers.

Scarcity beset rosé's popularity in the past: the good stuff was just not widely imported or retailed in the UK. This has changed. Thanks to the advent of the Internet, and the arrival of more perspicacious wine merchants, rosé is now much easier to get hold of.

Until a few years ago, even enlightened wine merchants would rarely stock more than one or two rosés of indifferent quality, and most big off-licence chains offered only a desultory choice of pink plonk. Compared to the ever-expanding shelves of reds and whites, rosés seemed shoved-in as an afterthought, a curiosity, almost a freak of viniculture, marginalised to dusty shelves at floor level along with obscure liquors and tonic beverages.

There were reasons for this reluctance: rosé sold slowly then, and its appeal was seasonal. Reds and whites could stay on the shelves year-round until they shifted, but rosés were seen as a summertime tipple: between September and May, all it did was hog valuable shelf space.

In restaurants good rosés were more likely to be found, but were seldom less than pricey. To be sure, many Italian eateries included a rosato on their wine lists to accompany the pasta and pizza, but the quality was variable and the wines were often carelessly kept and not well served. Most restaurateurs simply did not *understand* rosé, and knew little about pairing it with menu items.

Any rosé hunter over the age of 40 will know that prior to mid-1990s, good quality stuff was hard to track down. You might come across a dusty flask of Côtes de Provence pink at more adventurous booze chains, but nothing to match the range of styles and qualities now available both off- and online. In the old days, anyone wanting to drink pink in the comfort of their own homes had to lug it back from abroad. Why, they would wonder, do stores in Italy, France, and Spain offer dozens of pink wines, while in the UK there was next to zilch?

There were exceptions. Some specialist wine stores would stock a Tavel, say, or one of the Torres rosados; Bordeaux rosés could sometimes be found in the 'proper grown-up' wine merchants' retail outlets. One of the old high street chains (was it Peter Dominic?) intermittently stocked a delicious but sharp Listel rosé *gris* in the early 1980s.

A big breakthrough for UK rosé fans — in London and the south-east at least — was the arrival of the Nicolas chain. Here, at least, was a wine seller that took pinks seriously. A range of multifarious French rosés was prominently and attractively displayed on its halogen-lit shelves. Not just famous-domain Côtes de Provences, but rosés from other notable regions — even Corsica.

122

A little bit of rosé heaven landed wherever a branch of Nicolas opened. Yes, they were all quite expensive, but they were *reassuringly* expensive. Surely this proved to the rosé nay-sayers that such wines could qualify for a quality premium?

Now UK wine buyers have more choice than ever, from both generalist stores to niche players specialising in wines from specific countries, specific regions. This revolution has carried rosé along with it. Multiples such as Oddbins and Majestic stock many classy rosés, and they regularly appear in promotions and mixed cases. (Oddbins has representative rosés from almost all of the main wine-producing countries it stocks: Argentina, Australia, Chile, Spain, Greece, and of course, France).

Of the major producing countries, Italy's rosatos are still under-represented in UK stores (they are not common from online winesellers for that matter). (Pasqua's Bardolino Chiaretto crops up at the Whistle Stop convinience store chain found at airports and railway termini.)

On the Internet, specialist wine sellers have further extended the range and diversity of rosés available to UK consumers. They can be small, agile and focused in shaping the wines they supply; they can source wines directly from wineries — and even individual winemakers — for resale in quantities that would be too small for the bigger players to be involved with. This model suits rosé, where supply and demand do not justify bulk orders and stock reposits in bonded storage centres.

The big established incumbents are also endeavouring to turn cyberspace into a legitimate sales channel, of course. All the high-street multiples and supermarkets have Internet sites which are also stores where you can buy the same products found in their shops (and sometimes more). They face some of their most challenging retailing in the drinks sector.

Size is highly relative in cyberspacial terms, and does not necessarily bring compelling commercial advantages. With adroit website design, you can appear as big or as small as you want. As a result, the bigger players have felt it necessary to evolve more distinctive and even quirky retail identities in order to compete.

123

The Net may have made it easier for rosé fans to find their favourite wine, but there are still great pink wines to be found in small, independent wine shops that have no online presence and don't seem to like using the telephone, let alone email. Such outlets are always worth investigating — *Rosé Exposé* researchers are always being delighted by unexpected finds in unlikely places; it is not uncommonly the case that in less salubrious outlets, the rosé is one of the best quality wines on sale.

Buying wine off the Web is not to everyone's liking: obviously you need to have Internet access, and the wherewithal to meet the access costs of time spent online perusing the wines and making buying decisions that might otherwise take place in a 'bricks and mortar' store.

Your PC and browsing skills need to be resilient enough to work through clunky websites that often return misleading or incorrect information. You will have to be qualmless about providing your credit card details to electronic purchasing systems. But for punters who persevere, the results are very rewarding.

Dynamics of online buying

As with a conventional shop, online wine sellers each have their own approach to organising their wares: they might basically categorise their wine lists by colour, country of origin, region, grape varietal, price, and so on. They will also probably enable you to find what you want by using a site search function. This is helpful where a supplier has a huge range of wines, and where buyers do not have a huge amount of time to browse through them (most customers who buy online have an idea of what they are after).

It is impractical (but not impossible) for sellers to display entire ranges on a single web page. Standard browsers let you run keyword searches on individual web pages, but this is a laborious way of doing it. What's more, a searchable product database is regarded as a staple component of a serious online retail site.

So sellers try to help potential buyers find preferred wines by featuring denoted buttons that can be clicked on to take visitors through to their wines in a given category. You can search on two or more criteria at once – price and region, say – and narrow your search down by searching within the results of a previous search with different criteria. This is very useful when tracking-down rosés.

124

Some online sellers have a discrete rosé section listing pinks together; others lump rosés in with their reds or file them under 'Blushes'. Some seem to keep rosés in virtual limbo, not listed under any category, but only to be found by using the site's search engine by typing in 'rosé' or under the name of a specific rosé wine type. When trying to find rosé in a search engine always try with and without the accent — 'rosé' and 'rose' — some search engines recognise accents, others find them confusing. It is also worth repeating a search with and without capital Rs, though most search systems are case insensitive.

Some search results will present every wine with the letters r o s and e appearing sequentially in their names (e.g., Rosemount). You can also try rosado and rosato, as this will throw up pinks where the local term has been input as part of the wine's name. Do not completely accept the first set of results the search engine returns; try more searches using different terms. Rosés have a tendency to lurk on websites that do not explicitly categorise them.

Some wine sellers are starting to classify red and white wines by their 'heaviness' or 'density': for instance, Virgin Wines divides its reds into 'soft', 'juicy', 'classic', 'full', 'fruity', and 'huge' (not to mention 'lunchtime' reds). This is an interesting approach to classifying wine, and commendably egalitarian, but it is also a bit gimmicky.

Rosé Exposé has not found an online retailer applying such a criteria to rosés, although a similar approach to characterising wine body and density differences could prove very helpful to rosé novices. Despite the marked contrasts in rosé styles, most vendors sound like a stuck gramophone needle when it comes to ascribing the qualities to even their most distinctive pinks, using the same terms of reference – 'strawberry-scented', 'flavours of summer fruits', 'bursting with raspberry flavours' — again and again.

Tasting descriptions / 'winemaker's notes'
To what extent do potted descriptions of the degustatory and olfactory highlights influence wine buying decisions? Probably price, packaging, (populist) grape, and place of origin, are more influential factors. There's not much point in trying to describe a superior wine in 20 words, and such blurbs are unlikely to contain any qualifying remarks.

125

Alas, as far as rosés are concerned, tasting descriptions are often bland and reiterative. Phrases like those given above – 'strawberry-scented', 'flavours of summer fruits', 'bursting with raspberry scents' — abound. Sites that take their rosé descriptions seriously are few.

As is suggested in the Four Fruits Scale (see Chapter Eight) on the palate and the nose, rosés can offer a broad spectrum of tasting experiences and evocative reactions that very often have nothing to do with fruits, summer or otherwise. It is also true that such descriptions are equally applied to reds and whites, and the worst of them can emanate from the winemaker, not the wine seller.

Quantities
Buying online does not necessarily mean buying in bulk. All online winesellers we know of will deliver a minimum of one case (12 bottles). Some offer discounts for orders totalling above a certain amount – e.g., 10% off orders over £200, and combined with mixed cases, this gives

buyers a way to fine tune their purchases so that they can just push their total purchases over this discount threshold.

Of course, it sometimes makes sense to bulk buy if you discover a wine which you really like, because winesellers revise their lists all the time, and there's a possibility they might not be able to offer it in future. So if you've the room and the budget, buying four or five cases is a wise move.

Discounts

Most of the wine chains, off-licence chains, and supermarkets offer discounts. These vary from 5% to 15% per case; 10% used to be the average. Some shops vary discounts on a seasonal basis, or in regard to limited-period special offers. Discounts will probably be witheld on other special deals. Some suppliers apply discounts to mixed cases, some don't. Discounts should be deducted automatically in the billing process, but always check it has been done.

Payment

Online winesellers accept a variety of payment methods, but obviously prefer to transact via standard credit cards. People are becoming less and less worried about providing credit card details over the web; remember if the wine doesn't arrive, you don't pay for it. All deliveries should be tracked and signed for. (Virgin Wines claim that even if a consignment gets nicked off your doorstep it will replace it without quibble.)

Delivery charges

Delivery charges can deter people from ordering wine: some say that discounts on the wine itself are invalidated by delivery charges. This is probably not the best way to consider delivery charges; one should be happy to accept that the convenience of having a bulky, heavy commodity like wine delivered to wherever you want is worth paying a little extra for. And on balance, delivery charges for all kinds of items have never been cheaper.

All of the UK-based online winesellers *Rosé Exposé* has used or surveyed seem reasonable in their delivery charges. Some wine sellers always make a flat upfront charge for delivery, some charge according to order size or delivery location, and some don't charge for delivery at all. About £5 (sometimes less) is a typical delivery charge for 12 or more bottles. In relative terms, and taking into account the convenience, most delivery charges are reasonable, but should be borne in mind when deciding how much your budget will allow for the wine itself.

Obviously retailers who deliver *gratis* within certain areas are an advantage. If, like Majestic, they also offer a varied and enticing rosé range, you're onto a double-whammy.

Breakages
Any 'to-your-door' wineseller worthy of the name will pack their products in cardboard boxes specially designed to protect their contents in transit. Many use third-party couriers who are charged to take extra care with wine deliveries, and therefore breakages are actually relatively rare.

Most wine sellers will, in any event, replace genuinely accidental breakages without demur. They want your repeat business and wish to avoid anything minor that might sully your opinion of them.

Mixed cases
Wine sellers and wine consumers like the mixed case concept. Mixed cases can be packaged in a variety of styles and themes, and give 'butterfly imbibers' the opportunity to sample 12 different kinds of wine from any region, in any style. Because it is unusual for any wine seller to stock more than 12 different rosés, mixed cases of pink wines are pretty much self-selecting. However, some retailers do pre-selected rosé mixed cases, most often presented as 'summertime specials'.

Buying direct from estates

For many enthusiasts it is the ultimate wine-buying experience — purchasing directly from the producer, on their home soil! How do you beat the buzz of conversing with the people who actually created the pink liquid in your glass, seeing some of the vines that created the very grapes, and learning just why each wine tastes like it does? Simply tasting the wines, before you buy, in a ambient tasting room tucked away in the château or domain — or even a cave co-operative — is the highlight of visiting a wine-growing country for many holiday-makers.

At the same time, due to the number of wineries in the main wine-making areas of France, Spain, Italy and Australia, many would-be visitors are deterred, unsure as to which winery to visit, worried they will be pressured into buying wine they don't actually much like on tasting. Don't let these forebodings put you off. Don't be daunted by buying direct. The process is very straightforward.

The first rule is: you do not need to buy the wines you taste, so don't feel obliged to buy simply because you've tried them. To find out whether you like them or not before you commit financially, is the whole point of the exercise — not to necessarily secure a sale.

A winemaker will not tell you to scram because you say their wine isn't *quite* what you were looking for (i.e., like). Winemakers are giving out free samples all the time to all kinds of interested parties — neighbours, business associates, fellow winemakers, wholesalers, retailers and agents. It is common practice.

At the same time, be open-minded about trying new styles — sweet or dry, still or sparkling. Even within **128** the world of rosé there is such an enormous range of styles and tastes that every week you can sample something with characteristics unlike anything tried before. That's what makes discovering wine's best-kept secret so exciting —and plain good fun.

Rule number two is: you do not have to buy caseloads. While it is possible to buy individual bottles from producers, it is more normal to buy in threes, sixes, or dozens, depending on the type, style and price of the wine. For example, in France it is the norm to buy in cartons of six bottles for regular table wine, whereas rich, sweet dessert wines are often bought by the bottle, or in packs of three.

If you do want to buy by the litre, there are options. An alternative offered by many producers is to buy the wine in bulk — called *vrac* in French — direct from the tanks, wine that has not been bottled. Bring or buy your own plastic container which they then fill, petrol-pump style, from the tank; or often you can buy pre-packaged wine in a wine-box, usually re-sealable so it will keep the wine fresh for some weeks (if you can make it last that long). The French strongly believe that a wine's ability to retain drinkability following air contact is a sure sign of quality.

Usually these will be five- or 10-litre boxes, though there are exceptions to this rule — lower and higher — depending on the winery. Usually the bulk wine is that current year's vintage — young wine — that could be anything from 'table wine' standard through to full-blown regulated regional wine, such as an AOC in France.

In almost all cases it is an absolute bargain, often significantly less than half the price of the bottled equivalent, and almost certainly loads cheaper than what you might pay at home in the UK. And whereas, in red wines, it can be overly acidic — simply too young, under fermented — for many rosé wines it is the perfect way to buy and drink them.

The joys of good, cheap, fresh gluggable rosé have their limits. What you do lose-out on in buying bulk wine straight from the tank, as well as the ability to age a wine, is the whole ritual involved in bottled wine — the tactility of the bottle shape, the scrutiny of the label, the satisfying pop of the cork and — for many people — the memories that recall happy visits to foreign climes.

Before it starts sounding too sentimental, while the bulk wine is perfectly drinkable when you buy it, there is always a slight chance that a bottled wine might be corked on opening and undrinkable.

129

If the winery is just down the road then — apart from the immediate disappointment — it is not a problem to return the wine (always do if you can) and get a replacement or refund, but if it is now a thousand miles away you are left empty-handed, and with no option but to open a second bottle of wine and shrug-off the loss. If you have got a good deal on the wine, then it's worth risking a hit on the odd off bottle.

Don't be deceived by the cost factor. Buying bottled wine directly from a producer does not always guarantee the best price. It is often the case that they have sold a large quantity of one or more of their wines to a supermarket chain (such as Géant or Carrefour in France) at a very low price, and that, even with the mark-up from the shop, it still works out cheaper to buy it from the supermarket.

However, through experience, buying directly from the supplier gives you a far better chance of guaranteeing the

quality of the wine and avoiding the aforementioned disappointment of uncorking a corked wine. Not all supermarkets store their wines as well as they might.

The wine industry can be as ruthless and cut-throat as any
other commercial sector, but winemakers are, by and
large, pleasant, easy-going and friendly folk. They are passionate about what they produce, and love discussing it.

Understanding labels and the rosé designations

"What do I look for on a wine label?" — this is the most
common question asked by wine consumers looking to
guarantee the quality of their purchases. Most wine labels
are not conspicuously user-friendly. Although they are all
supposed to be saying the same thing, they do so in a mul-
titude of ways that can easily confuse.

130 Information on a wine label is typically arranged in a
hierarchy. Understanding how this hierarchy is arranged is the key to identifying the rosé wines that
appeal to you.

"What *should* I look for in a wine label?" The answer first
depends on the country of origin, and second, on the style
of rosé you are looking to buy, the obvious example here
being that sparkling rosés carry different — or additional — information to still (no bubbles) wine.

Take France as a primary example. The whole wine industry is governed by a set of regulations called the Appellation Origine Controlée — AOC (or sometimes AoC). The
idea here is that the character of the land — the *terroir* —
defines what is best grown there, so different regions are
made to grow different grape types, thereby creating a
very wide range of tastes and styles within the one country. Within the dictates of the AOC system, not only are
specific grape types limited, but also the maximum percentage of any one grape type you are allowed to use, in
order to call that wine a specific AOC wine, such as Tavel
or Côtes de Provence. Any wine that falls outside of those
categories cannot be called an AOC wine. There is a secon-
dary level — VDQS (Vin Delimité de Qualité Superieur) —

which is for those regions looking to become AOC rated but not having yet been listed as AOC. For example, many of the AOC wines you drink, such as Corbières and Minervois, have only become AOC classified relatively recently, having been VDQS rated for many years before that.

VDQS wines are also regulated in AOC style, so there is a guarantee of 'authenticity' with this classification. Within an AOC area, there are also many wines produced using the non-approved grape types and these are usually classified as Vin de Pays wines, a very popular example being Vin de Pays d'Oc.

Many of these Vin de Pays wines are actually excellent quality but simply do not conform to the AOC standard. As such they are often bargains as there is a degree of snobbery and pricing related to an AOC classification. That said, in recent times there has been a movement — an inverse snobbery — towards producing absolute top-quality wines which can only attain Vin de Pays status because of the grape types used. This becomes even more extreme with certain Vin de Table (table wine) wines (the classification designated generally for the lowest quality wines in France — often EC wine-lake blends) which can be of terrifically high quality (with matching price tags).

131

To outsiders the French wine classification system seems like a morass of bureaucracy, but its purpose is governed by a desire to preserve the integrity of French winemaking's best traditions by preventing unscrupulous winemakers mucking about with the rules of quality.

That said, there are winemakers who are exemplars of the ideals of quality who have opted to work outside of the official classification system; these wine rebels — some have been dubbed 'The Wild Bunch' by wine author Patrick Matthews in his book of the same name — work to their own rules because they find the official system constraining. Nobody's knocking the quality of their wines.

Italy follows a similar scheme with its DoC (Denominazione di Origine Controllata) classification system with many of the best wines being Vino di Tavola (Vin de Table) rated because of the grape types being used. Spain and Portugal have similar 'DOC' systems in place place, with similar loopholes allowing high quality wines to be produced with supposedly 'inferior' label tags. Typically the price will dictate whether this is a genuine (low-end) table wine or an unclassified but excellent (and relatively or very expensive) wine.

And then there is often little on the European wine label to tell you what grapes are used to make the wine. New World wines, meanwhile, tend toward a more explicit approach — generally signalling the region of produce and the grape types used in the wine, on the label or on an additional back label. However, European wine labels still tend to only inform you of the region and classification of that wine, though this is changing slowly, notably with 'Vin de Pays' or equivalent level wines.

Consequently, it helps if you know something about the classification systems of each country, region by region, and the grape types that are allowed to be used in that region, in order to help guess what the wine is made up of, and how it is likely to taste. This is no easy matter, and usually only comes with years of experience in the business. A short-cut on French AOC rosés to help with the basics can be found at the end of Chapter Three.

132

Taking the French example again, one clue as to the quality of the wine, whether AOC, VDQS or Vin de Pays, is whether or not it is château/domaine bottled. Many wines, even AOC classified, are not bottled at source — i.e., the winery making the wine — but at an independent bottling plant, often a giant hissing and clanking industrial concern, the nature of which can be directly linked with the quality of the wine itself.

While château/domaine-bottled wine is still not guaranteed to be excellent wine, it is a pointer in the right direction. In addition to the label, on the bottle itself you may see a sticker pronouncing the wine as a medal winner (bronze, silver or gold). Again, this acts as a positive pointer towards the wine being above average, even if some awards are not exactly regarded within the industry as being worth the paper they are printed upon.

French restaurants & rosé

In France, rosé is commonly available in restaurants and bistros, either by the jug *pichet* or by the bottle. Notably in the lower-priced restaurants, house wines are usually served by the jug (quarter, half or litre) and usually just red or rosé are available in this format.

This means that, especially on the daytime menus, rosé is effectively a replacement for white wine and is the common lunchtime and early evening tipple in France. It actually goes better with a lot of seafood than most whites do, especially cheap whites which tend towards the cheap 'n' nasty. The cheap rosé, on the other hand, is always in the 'gluggable' category. It is also very, very inexpensive — cheaper than mineral water in many a UK restaurant.

As you would expect, in regional France the bottled rosés on offer reflect what is available in the local area. So, in the Corbières, for example, you will be offered Corbières rosés, in the Loire, Loire rosés, in the Rhône, Rhône and Tavel rosés and so on. Where there are no local rosés made, or it is a non-winemaking region of France, expect to see the classics — notably rosés from Côtes de Provence — on the menu, unless the restaurateur has a particular favourite region.

133

The great label debate

What can be done to make wine drinkers try more rosé? It's not entirely down to introducing them to a range of quality pink wines wide enough to contain something to suit all palates. Making wine attractive encompasses multiple aspects. Aside from 'inhibitors' such as the 'Mateus Legacy' and perceptions of immasculinity associated with pink drink, rosé can also be affected by an issue for wines of all hues from around the world: labels.

You may be indifferent to wine, but everyone likes to have an opinion about wine labels. The question of labels – what they should look like, what they should impart — arouses heated debate in 'wine circles' for reasons that might seem obtuse, if not a bit silly, to outsiders. A wine bottle's label is the wine's public face to the world, and *ipso facto*, the market.   *Continues overleaf*

Continued
Although many winemakers say label considerations are incidental to what they do, and that it is the wine on the other side of the glass that is the most important thing (quite true), there's no doubt that the label's appearance will in many cases influence whether a consumer picks up the bottle in the first place. This is especially apposite to rosé, which is attracting a higher proportion of younger drinkers looking for a 'lifestyle' tipple.

Labels should indicate something about the winemaker's ethos. Some long-established names opt for a classic look, with stately typography and graphics depicting the château or vineyard; big wine concerns like to festoon their labels with branded icons and logos; others go for a more modernistic or contemporary look, commissioning artists to create striking images to decorate labels.

Others still prefer the minimalist approach, with labels carrying the minimum (even a deficit) of information about the bottle's contents.

134 All such approaches (and others beside) are prone to the same complaint from wine sellers and wine buyers: they do not provide enough clear information about the wine. In recent years many winemakers have added another label on the back of the bottle containing such information, plus a few sloppy marketing slogans.

Some 'old school' winemakers regard these as downmarket fripperies, pandering to the wine hoi polloi. This seems disingenuous, as labels are surely the primary source for acquiring a knowledge, understanding and appreciation of wine.

Some winemakers are guilty of a certain hauteur when it comes to divulging details about the origins of their wines. They expect potential customers to know everything about their products by reputation it seems, and may not even name the grape varieties used, let alone information about the environmental characteristics of the vineyard – or part of the vineyard – where the wine's grapes were grown. And explaining the basics of the production methods used strikes them as absurd, even possibly equivalent to divulging trade secrets.

PRODUCT OF FRANCE

M A S ——————— 1

MOURIES

M

VIN DE PAYS D'OC ——————— 2

6 ——————— 2001

5 ———————   *Mis en bouteille par*   ——————— 3

4

1. The name of the Producer/Wine
2. The denomination and geographical region
3. The quantity of wine in the bottle
4. Bottler and (usually) where it was bottled
5. The alcohol level
6. The vintage (year of harvest)

There is, of course, no shortage of reliable information about wine and its whys and wherefores; but not all wine enthusiasts set out with a copy of the latest wine guides stuffed into their bags and pockets. When they come across a new and enjoyable wine, they want to learn something about it there and then, at the moment of tasting, and the label would seem to be the best place for such an exposition.

We are all willing to do a bit of research to this end. Increasingly winemakers and wineries have websites where more detailed information may (or may not) be found; these should at least provide an email address for direct enquiries. Winemakers love to hear from the people who enjoy their wines, so don't worry about being snubbed. If no Internet address is given on the label, always try running the wine/winemaker name through a standard Internet search engine – it's not unknown for winemakers to forget to include it.

Appendix

UK sellers of rosé

T his guide is selective. The list does not define a market, or propose the UK's top rosé wine sellers. These are simply suppliers who have been found to be offering quality wines at reasonable prices. New rosé sellers are appearing all the time – and new rosés. The details were correct at time of going to press (March 2003). All suppliers are revising their stock lists all the time; for this reason we have avoided stating retail prices. Submit editorial information for future editions to info@rose-expose.com.

Wine chains / off-licences

Majestic Wine
Probably the UK's largest wine warehouse chain with 103 outlets. Majestic sells mainly by the case only, but home delivery is free within a reasonable distance of a Majestic store. Majestic's rosé selection changes, but during the 2002/2003 season, it offered around 11 outstanding specimens, including an Italian (Chiaretto, Cavalchina Bardolino). Unlike its main rivals, Majestic offers one or two higher end (£7+) pinks, such as Château de Sours Bordeaux Rosé, and, Domaine Roger Neveu Sancerre Rosé. In store, Majestic groups rosés together which makes buying slightly easier.
www.majestic.co.uk

Oddbins
A brand stalwart in any UK high street with around 240 stores, Oddbins rosé range is narrower and less upmarket than other players, but its global reach in rosé terms is greater: pinks from France, Spain, Chile, Australia, Argentina, South Africa and Greece. All the wines are worth trying, although not all are outstanding.
www.oddbins.com

Unwins
The UK's 'largest family owned independent wine merchant', with over 400 shops in the South of England, Unwins carries only three rosés, and then not in every branch. One of these is the outstanding Domaine Méjan Tavel, 2001 (as featured on the cover of *Rosé Exposé*); also noteworthy is the J.P. Chenet Cinsault Rosé, 2001. Unwins also carries a basic Les Trois Rosé, which although mediocre in style represents good value.

Nicolas

Nicolas has around 20 stores dotted in and around central London. It sells the best and broadest range of quality French rosés you are likely to find within the UK, with famous domains and regional stars represented – but beware that their prices reflect their high quality, though are by no means exorbitant. Less expensively, Nicolas also sells a range of 'house' rosés of good quality. All Nicolas wines are displayed with finesse. Its staff – usually French – are knowledgeable and affable. Nicolas' problem at the moment is a confused and confusing online 'strategy' (two sites, the .co.uk one in dire need of updating) which needs to be addressed if it is interested in establishing its credibility in this sphere.

www.nicolas-wines.com, www.nicolas.co.uk

Supermarket chains

Asda

Fairly mediocre rosé range with a bias toward undistinguished Portuguese and US brands, but the Valdivieso Malbec Chilean rosé is worth trying.

www.asda.com

140

Booths

Northern England chain has some respectable pinks among its rosés that its bigger rivals would do well to study: in particular, the Château Lamothe Vincent Bordeaux Rosé, Castillo de Maluenda Rosado, Bardolino Chiaretto Cavalchina.

www.booths-wine.co.uk

Budgen

Budgen has dallied with better-quality rosés in recent years, and some fair-quality varieties have passed across its shelves at some time or another. But current evidence suggests that the company has reached the conclusion that Budgen customers aren't keen on the pink stuff. A notable exception in selected stores is a Kumala rosé from South Africa. Budgen's website is under construction.

Co-Op / Co-Op2U

A range of 10 rosés, each under £5. Includes the redoubtable Bulgarian Valley of the Roses, and an Argentinean pink from Bodegas Baldi.

www.co-op2u.com

Sainsbury's

Sainsbury's wine focus is arguably the best of the UK 'big five' supermarkets, and in rosé terms it scores well in most stores. Its Cuvée Victoria, Rosé de Provence is good and drinkable but a tad overpriced. Other pinks to look out for are Inycon Rosé, Cabernet-Sauvignon — a rare Rosato di Sicilia – and Arniston Bay Rosé from South Africa. Its rosé range could do with one or two real crackers to put it ahead of its rivals in the pink stakes.

www.sainsbury.co.uk

Safeway

Good international range of medium-quality rosés: pinks from Bulgaria, Hungary, Argentina, Spain, and the US (the rather insipid Lake Pyramid, Napa Gamay). An outstanding French rosé would augment the range nicely.

www.safeway.co.uk

Somerfield

A succinct rosé range with a bias toward Spanish labels, though its Goûts et Couleurs Cinsault Rosé, Fontcaude looks like a worthy contender.

www.somerfield.co.uk

Tesco

141

A range of pinks from France, Australia, Argentina, and Spain, but mostly branded under the Tesco banner, and mostly pretty much positioned at budget levels of price and quality. Tesco is introducing two rosés of note in 2003, the Antipodean Sangiovese Rosé 2002, and Tesco Unwind Rosé, also sourced from Australia, from Rutherglen Estates – a well-balanced compendium blend of Shiraz (40%), Durif (25%), Sangiovese (15%), Grenache (8%), Mourvdre (8%), and Sauvignon Blanc (4%).

www.tesco.com

Waitrose

The John Lewis Partnership's grocery chain's two stars to date were the Château de Caraguilhes Rosé from Corbières, and Crémant de Bourgogne Rosé, Lugny – a superb sparkler. However, Waitrose will be introducing some new rosés for the Spring of 2003. They include: Cuvée Fleur Rosé 2002, Vin de Pays de l'Hérault, Domaine de Pellehaut 2002, Vin de Pays des Côtes de Gascogne; La Baume Syrah Rosé 2002, Vin de Pays d'Oc; and the excellent Château La Moutète 2002, Côtes de Provence.

www.waitrose.com

Online suppliers of rosé

Each of the following Internet wine sellers offer good quality rosés worth investigating – visit them directly, or view the BestDealsIndex on www.drink-pink.com for a overview of their wines. Some of these companies also have retail stores.

Best Cellars — www.bestcellars.co.uk

Bon Coeur Fine Wine — www.bcfw.co.uk

Booths — www.booths-wine.co.uk

Case Value — www.casevalue.com

Chateau Online — www.uk.chateauonline.com

Compendium Wines — www.compendiumwines.com

Devigne Wines — www.devignewines.co.uk

Duncan Murray Wines

— www.duncanmurraywines.co.uk

Everywine — www.everywine.co.uk

142

Floyd On Wine — www.floydonwine.com

Gauntley Wine — www.gauntley-wine.co.uk

Wine Raks — www.wineraks.com

Laithwaites — www.laithwaites.co.uk

London Fine Wine – www.londonfinewine.co.uk

Oxford Wine Company — www.oxfordwine.co.uk

Rioja Wine Club — www.riojawineclub.co.uk

Roberson Wine Merchant – www.roberson.co.uk

Rouge & Blanc – www.rouge-blanc.com

Sunday Times Wine Club

— www.sundaytimeswineclub.co.uk

Virgin Wines — www.virginwines.com

Whitebridge Wines — www.whitebridgewines.co.uk

Wine Alive — www.winealive.com

Wine From Spain — www.wine-from-spain.com

Independent wine shops

There are loads, but here are just a few of those based in and around central London that Rosé Exposé *researchers have tried and like.*

Gerry's Wines & Spirits

Gerry's has been a beacon for West End rosé rustlers for decades. Two rosés worth sampling are a Navarran, Orvalaiz Cabernet-Sauvignon rosado and from France, Domaine de Gournier, a Vin De Pays Des Cévennes. Gerry's also stocks the Mouton Cadet Bordeaux Rosé. You'll have to pay in cash — Gerry's does not accept credit cards. Address: 74 Old Compton Street, London W1V 5PA. Tel: 0207 734 4215.

SH Jones & Co

Long-established family wine merchant. Does two rosés of high merit: Château de Fonscolombe rosé and a Sancerre pink, Les Celliers Saint-Romble from *vignerons* André Dezat et Fils. Banbury branch is at The Old Wine House, 27 High Street. Banbury. OX16 8EW. The Bicester branch is at 9 Market Square, Bicester, Oxfordshire OX6 7AA.

143

Lea & Sandeman

Helmed by Charles Lea and Partick Sandeman, L. & S. offers an exquisitely-chosen range of wines, featuring several prominent pinks. L&S has branches at: 170 Fulham Road, London SW10 9PR (020 7244 0522), 211 Kensington Church Street, London W8 7LX (020 7221 1982), 51 High Street, Barnes, London SW13 9LN (020 8878 8643), 206 Haverstock Hill, London NW3 2AG (020 7431 4412). Lea & Sandeman wines are also sold via the Internet from London Fine Wine – www.londonfinewine.co.uk.

Roberson Wine Merchant

Situated toward the Olympia end of Kensington High Street (no. 348), Roberson's extensive includes some top-notch French rosés, namely Château Recougne Bordeaux Superieur, Domaine de la Berle Provence, Sancerre Dezat Loire, and Sancerre Rosé Les Baronnes Henri Bourgeois. But the real star is Domaine Ott Coeur de Gain Provence) — one of the priciest pinks you will find this side of the Channel. The Lebanese Château Musar Rosé is also available. Tel: 0207 371 2121. Www.roberson.co.uk.

Soho Wine Supply

Established in 1890, Soho Wine Supply, based just off Tottenham Court Road, stocks at least four rosés of merit: a stalwart Bordeaux, Château le Preuil 2000, and a Spaniard, Condesa de Leganza (2000), a 100% Tempranillo grape rosado from the Finca los Trenzones, Toledo. The Torres rosé duo – de Casta and Santa Digna – also share the shelves. The information on the SWS website is a bit sketchy. Address: 18 Percy Street, London W1P 9FE. www.sohowine.co.uk

The Vintage House

A Soho institution for over 20 years, the Vintage House mainly caters to lovers of fine reds and whiskies, but also carries a few better rosés. Notable among them is Mouton Cadet Bordeaux rosé from the estate of Baron Philippe de Rothschild. Also stocked is the Torres de Casta rosado. Credits cards accepted only for purchases of £15 and over. Address: 42 Old Compton Street, London W1V 6LR. Tel: 0207 437 2592.

Wine Bargains of North London

With one of the most eclectic wine ranges you will find in the locale, Wine Bargains of North London is within easy reach of the Holborn and Clerkenwell districts.

144

A notable recent arrival is the sublime Abbaye Saint-Hilaire Côteaux Varois Rosé, 2001. Also stocked is the Bardolino Chiaretto from the renowned Pasqua house of Italy. Address: Leather Lane, London, EC1N 7TR. Also rosés from Portugal and Chile. Tel: 0207 404 9625.

Acknowledgements

Many thanks to Susan for her work on Rosé Exposé and her love and support along with Becky, Sam and Tom.

Thanks to Steve's parents, family and friends for more love and support, and to The Landlord for putting up with us.

Thanks also to Jane Dudman for her valuable help in editing the MS. and spirited assistance in researching the subject matter.

The help of the many winemakers and wine industry folk who provided information and encouragement for Rosé Exposé is gratefully acknowledged.

145

Index

Index

149

151

152